RACE AN
RESISTA

South End Press
Cambridge, Massachusetts

RACE AND RESISTANCE

African Americans in the Twenty-First Century

Herb Boyd, Editor

South End Press
Cambridge, Massachusetts

Any properly footnoted quotation of up to 500 sequential words may be used without permission, as long as the total number of words quoted does not exceed 2,000. For longer quotations or for a greater number of total words, please write to South End Press for permission.

Cover design by Ellen Shapiro.
Printed in Canada by Transcontinental Printing.

Library of Congress Cataloging-in-Publication Data

Race and Resistance ; African-Americans in the twenty-first century / edited by Herb Boyd.
   p. cm.
   Includes bibliographical references and index.
   ISBN 0-89608-653-4 (alk. paper) — ISBN 0-89608-652-6 (pbk. : alk.. paper)
      1. African Americans—Politics and government—21st century. 2. African Americans—Social Conditions—21st century. 3. African Americans—Race identity. 4. United States—Race relations. 5. United States—Race relations—Political aspects. 6. United States—Politics and government—2001- I. Boyd, Herb, 1938-

E185.615.R21215 2002
305.896'073—dc21

                                    2002070573

South End Press, 7 Brookline Street, #1
Cambridge, MA 02139-4146
www.southendpress.org

06 05 04 03 02   1 2 3 4 5

Table of Contents

Acknowledgments

Of all the sections in a book, the acknowledgments may be the most challenging. Invariably, some key people are overlooked as you rush to include those who have contributed mightily to the project. Knowing this risk, let me say at the outset that this collection would not be under my editorial guidance without a fortunate meeting with Lynn Lu at a Socialist Scholars conference a few years ago. It was at her urging that I took this assignment and while she has moved on to other pursuits, she provided the first spark. Subsequently, it was Anthony Arnove who nursed the embers until Jill Petty arrived and really applied the bellows. She was a tireless worker and indispensable.

Indispensable, too, are the roster of writers assembled here. They represent the best of the thinkers, scholars, and activists on the various topics they discuss, and I owe them big time.

As with all my writing endeavors, there is a coterie of informants—some of whom I talk to daily—who keep me in touch with the world of struggle. Don Rojas, Robert Van Lierop, Marie Brown, Clarence Atkins, Elinor Tatum, Minister Conrad Muhammad, Playthell Benjamin, Bob Belden, Todd Burroughs, Danny Aldridge, Cleophus Roseboro, Elombe Brath, Michael Dinwiddie, Ron Daniels, Charles Moore, Yvonne Bynoe, Chris Griffith, John Binion, Ron Lockett, David Ritz, Paul Lee, Malik Edwards, Jules Allen, Bill Katz, Robert Allen, and my mother, Katherine Brown, are among the host of callers and called who provide sustenance to mind, body, and the body politic.

When I work as a journalist it is the messages of the Rev. Al Sharpton, Johnnie Cochran, Russell Simmons, Charles Ogletree, Linn Washington, Dr. Leonard Jeffries, Imhotep Gary Byrd, Dr. James McIntosh, Betty Dodson, Howard Dodson, Alton Maddox, Molefi Asante, Viola Plummer, Dr. James Turner, Conrad Worrill, Richard Muhammad, Evette Porter, Victoria Valentine, Aziz Ademiterin, Akiba Solomon—some as informants, some as subjects—who are critical to my survival in the new world order as well as the "new word order."

The academy provides me with other resourceful contacts, particularly The College of New Rochelle and New York University, where I continue to serve as an adjunct instructor. My associates at these institutions—Dr. Louis De Salle, Sharwyn Dyson, Ernest Crane, Sam Lilly, Mary Witty, et al—provide a scholarly counterweight to the cadre of activists who spend their time on the ramparts of social and political change.

While I was mulling over the topics and contributors to this collection, I traveled to the Middle East where once more it was possible to see first hand the brutal disregard for human life in the seemingly unending cycle of violence between the Israeli government and the Palestinian people. Far less violent was a journey to Durban, South Africa to participate in the World Conference Against Racism. There it was possible to confer with a brigade of top thinkers on racism, the Atlantic slave trade, and reparations. Later, trips to Atlanta to participate in the State of the Black World Conference and the launching of the Institute of the Black World afforded me opportunities to touch base with several of the contributors, including Ron Daniels, Sonia Sanchez, and Julianne Malveaux.

During a similar jaunt to Los Angeles for a task force on the Black media as a delegate from *The Black World Today,* I was thoroughly informed on the HIV/AIDS crisis by Phill Wilson, his staff, and other participants. I depended a great deal on meeting allies and contributors at rallies, summits, symposiums, and conferences to solidify the objectives of *Race and Resistance.*

Thanks to writers Don Rojas, Carl Dix, Abdul Alkalimat, Danny Aldridge, and Safiyah Bukhari, who played crucial roles at the beginning of this process. Their thoughtful perspectives on the Internet as a tool for social change, police brutality, Black Studies, the new spirituality, and the plight of political prisoners informed this anthology. Their time and consideration is deeply appreciated.

Let me extend my gratitude to the collective at South End Press who helped shape this project with their customary verve and insight. Thanks also to David Barsamian, producer of Alternative Radio, who granted permission for us to reprint speeches by Amiri Baraka and Ron Daniels in the anthology.

I would have all of the above know how important they are in my life, and I would have them know the importance of my ever dependable companion, Elza, who makes it possible for me to work the streets, the rallies, conferences and workshops, while she holds our home together.

...It is essential that we finally understand:
this is the time for the creative
human being
the human being who decides
to walk upright in a human
fashion in order to save this
earth from extinction.

This is the time for the creative
Man. Woman. Who must decide
that She. He. Can live in peace.
Racial and sexual justice on
this earth.

This is the time for you and me.
African Americans. Whites. Latinos.
Gays. Asians. Jews. Native
Americans. Lesbians. Muslims.
All of us must finally bury
the elitism of race superiority
the elitism of sexual superiority
the elitism of economic superiority
the elitism of religious superiority...

—Sonia Sanchez
from *Shake Loose My Skin: New and Selected Poems*
(Boston: Beacon Press, 1999)

Introduction

While many of the issues facing African Americans at the beginning of the twenty-first century are not novel, our strategies for self-determination, expression, and indeed, resistance, have had to be consistently inventive and resourceful to be effective. Whether through coalition-building, music, poetry, or frontline activism, the contributors to this anthology dip in the well of theory and practice that has nourished generations of African American activists and invent new ways to challenge the status quo.

Political activist Ron Daniels places the topic of resistance within the broad context of American history. He explores how the social phenomenon of racism remains as oppressive and venal today as it was during the days of the "peculiar institution."

Daniels traces the challenging trajectory faced by African Americans in this last century: the violent and repressive aspects of Jim Crow, the exclusionary policies of the labor movement, the systematic denial of human rights by the legal and political establishments, and the reversals of affirmative action and other civil rights legislation during the Reagan era. As Daniels observes, there are tremendous obstacles to overcome, but African American progressives and our allies can draw from the bravery of those "agitators" who came before us. "We are those who struggled in the civil rights movement and made significant gains," he reminds. "We are the people who blocked the war in Vietnam, stopped it."

When you consider the history of African Americans, it is important to examine how and why we were ripped from Africa in the first place, and what the impact of that captivity has been. Labor activist Bill Fletcher tackles this issue with insight during an interview conducted last year, when he was an assistant to President John Sweeney of the AFL-CIO. (Fletcher is now the director of

TransAfrica.) The treatment Blacks have received in the labor movement is representative of how Blacks have fared in the society at large. As in most social and cultural institutions in the nation, Blacks were largely excluded from organized labor, and where they were accepted they were exploited and consigned to the rank and file.

After the Civil War, Fletcher observes, Black workers began to fight for justice, playing vital roles in numerous strikes. It was during this period that the labor movement was divided between a more open and liberal wing and a section that was exclusive and restrictive. Fletcher deftly charts the shifting realities of Black workers from the 1930s through the 1960s, a productive phase that witnessed the rise of Black leadership beyond the pulpit. He submits a brief but revealing analysis of the radical movements formed by Black workers with a particular emphasis on the League of Revolutionary Black Workers, an organization based in Detroit during the turbulent sixties.

Fletcher discusses globalization, welfare reform, the Black middle class, and the strengths and weaknesses of the Black Radical Congress, in which he was a founding member, as they relate to Black workers. On the history and evolution of the Black Radical Congress (BRC), we offer two essays. Professor Manning Marable, who like Fletcher was a co-founder, provides an account of the organization from its inception in 1996–97. At the core of the organization was the aim to promote dialogue among African American activists and scholars on the left, to discuss critical issues on the national and international front, and to explore strategies and tactics for progressive political, social, and cultural movements. In short, it was a grand attempt to rejuvenate the movement of the sixties and early seventies with an impetus on operational unity and with the realization that the mistakes of the past could be avoided, particularly the ideological differences that created several sectarian splits.

"Fresh thinking and creative approaches are required to overcome class exploitation, racism, sexism, homophobia, to protect the environment and to build a humane and just society in a peaceful world," the BRC's mission statement proclaimed. But, as in most instances, one cannot jettison the baggage of the past so easily, and some of the political problems that plagued the Black left "back in the day" are beginning to rear their ugly, divisive heads once more. Some of BRC's successes and failures are illuminated with compassion and precision by Jennifer Hamer and Clarence Lang, both BRC stalwarts. Theirs is a critical, constructive analysis that observes: "Despite its resources, emancipatory vision, and agenda, the BRC sorely lacks a coordinated strategy for implementing any practical program." Compromises on critical issues, the national leadership's inability to execute a coherent plan of action, and the lack of resources and ingenuity to maintain more than a few local organizing committees are among the obstacles that hinder the growth and effectiveness of the organization, the writers assert.

Hamer and Lang suggest that the BRC, though blessed with a number of resourceful individuals, has lacked the resolve to deal with internal conflicts or to determine how funds should be raised to sustain the group. It also lacks a process through which to mollify the contradictions and schisms that have surfaced in the youth and feminist caucuses. Some of these setbacks, they suggest, might have been avoided had the organization and its various components adhered more closely to the Principles of Unity and the Freedom Agenda.

Unity, freedom, and sustained reform efforts might also help the Black church, Minister Paul Scott asserts. While the Black church and its more prophetic ministers have been indispensable in the struggle for liberation, the church may also have a tendency to be hidebound and mired in conventional values, hewing to a conservative outlook that blocks possibilities for progressive change. What is needed in the church, Scott declares, is an African Reformation Movement. "There have been reformation movements initiated by Europeans," he writes, "but since we've been taught that Christianity is a gift from the white man, some of us have not felt that we have the spiritual authority to change a thing. We have accepted the religion as is."

Scott is proposing a church in keeping with the zeal of a David Walker, Bishop Henry McNeal Turner or Nat Turner, even a Dr.

Martin Luther King, Jr. In this era of faith-based initiatives, we can be thankful for Johnny Ray Youngblood, Herb Daughtry, Michael Eric Dyson, Wyatt Tee Walker, Suzanne Johnson-Cooke, Calvin Butts, and Al Sharpton, who with their separate agendas are busy dealing with some of the social and political demons that are the progeny of what Dr. King called "interpositions and nullifications."

Noted activist Angela Davis offers detailed information about the profit-making role of the prison industrial complex. "Many corporations whose products we consume on a daily basis have learned that prison labor power can be as profitable as third world labor power exploited by US-based global corporations," Davis explains. "Both relegate formerly unionized workers to joblessness and many even wind up in prison. Some of the companies that use prison labor are IBM, Motorola, Compaq, Texas Instruments, Honeywell, Microsoft, and Boeing. But it is not only the high-tech industries that reap the profits of prison labor. Nordstrom department stores sell jeans that are marketed as 'Prison Blues,' as well as T-shirts and jackets made in Oregon prisons. The advertising slogan for these clothes is 'made on the inside to be worn on the outside.' Maryland prisoners inspect glass bottles and jars used by Revlon and Pierre Cardin, and schools throughout the world buy graduation caps and gowns made by South Carolina prisoners."

Rather than constructing more prisons, Davis proposes better education, more health care, affordable housing, and drug programs to treat the addicted instead of punishing them with unfair prison sentences. "The prison industrial complex has thus created a vicious cycle of punishment which only further impoverishes those whose impoverishment is supposedly 'solved' by imprisonment," Davis observes. Building more jails than schools is not the answer to this problem, she insists. Her declaration echoes the BRC's plan of action—"education not incarceration."

As forms of communication become faster, subtler, and more pervasive, African Americans must find new ways to combat or at least counter the negative, distorted images about their social, cultural, and political realities in this country. Alice Tait and Todd Burroughs are diligent media analysts and commentators who understand the profound effect of the media.

Tait and Burroughs give considerable attention to the electronic media, which, given the comparatively greater number of hours Black children spend watching television, makes a lot of sense. They also point out the deplorable lack of Black-owned media: Black Entertainment Television (BET), for example, has a monopoly on cable television and seems content to inundate viewers with rap videos and scarcely any news or public affairs programming. If there is to be any true challenge to the seemingly inevitable merging of the media into one or two oppressive entities, it may spring from the consolidation of progressive alternative media on the Internet, Tait and Burroughs propose.

Raptivist Chuck D offers similarly cogent advice in Yvonne Bynoe's essay on the impact of hip hop culture, where the author compares many contemporary rap artists to modern-day minstrels. Even so, Bynoe urges, to dismiss hip hop culture is to ignore the latest phase of African American orality and discount a generation's reflection on the social and political impositions that stifle growth and awareness. Resisting the temptation to oversimplify the evolution of rap music, she is cognizant of the two polarities of "commercial" and "conscious" rap, with the former, hardcore variety controlled by market forces. She also deftly dissects the reasons why hip hop culture has not evolved into a political movement. "Although individual artists and groups are political, a long-standing criticism of hip hop is that it has not generated a sustainable political movement," she explains. "The criticism is somewhat illogical since overt political engagement was not hip hop's *raison d'etre*. Rap music began as community entertainment and any political function was largely subtextual or incidental. Before any large-scale movement can be contemplated, the post–civil rights generation would first have to build a viable political apparatus just as the Black Arts Movement was the sister organization to the Black Power Movement. Hip hop is a cultural expression whereas politics is concerned with influencing governmental policy." Hip hop culture, she insists, is inextricably connected to the youthful exuberance of previous decades, "a metaphor" of their times, and to vilify this cultural expression is to relegate an entire generation to the dustbin of history.

Misogyny, which abounds in rap music in that way that "moon" and "June" used to dominate the song lyrics of another age, has been particularly disturbing to Black feminists. This bashing of women—in the regular references to "bitches and ho's" among top rap artists— is demeaning and destructive, and is facing increasing criticism and resistance in the Black community. Some of this resistance is articulated by Joy James' essay. In "Resting in Gardens, Battling in Deserts," James reconstructs the stereotypical portrayals of Black women that draw on fetishistic and sexualized imagery. Among the various branches of Black feminist theory and praxis, James opts for a radical form. "Of the many branches of Black feminisms extending from battles for a liberated African and female existence in America, the most imaginative and transformative take root in Black female radicalism," she writes. "It is impossible here to offer a comprehensive survey of the ideological diversity or plurality of Black feminist activisms, or the more subtle differences found even within radical Black feminism. Yet it is essential that we examine the limits of liberalism or civil rights advocacy, as well as Black women's challenges to state power and antiradicalism within conventional feminist and antiracist politics." James' remarks on Black women's incarceration complement the discussions about the prison industrial complex by Davis, and her brief observations about the power of the word in the arsenal of such poets/writers as Sonia Sanchez, Audre Lorde, Alice Walker, and Toni Cade Bambara anticipate Amiri Baraka's essay in this volume.

In "Riffin' on Music and Language," Baraka explores the key elements of African American culture, such as the blues and jazz, that can be traced to traditional West African *griot* and *djali* musicians and performers. To Baraka, a griot of considerable prowess, these cultural workers were not just entertainers and storytellers but custodians of memory. They are the link in the transatlantic chain leading to Louis Armstrong, Bessie Smith, Miles Davis, Gil Scott-Heron, and modern-day rappers. Baraka's conclusions about the potential of cultural expression to politicize are similar to those

offered by Bynoe, which indicates that the gulf between generations may not be as yawning as we often assume.

Regardless of the differences between the baby boomers and
hip hoppers, there seems to be cross-generational agreement on
the necessity of reparations. The first class action suit was filed by
advocates and plaintiffs of reparations against three major corporations in 2002, and the subject has commanded media attention.
But for a number of veteran Black activists, this demand on behalf
of African captives who toiled for hundreds of years and seasons
without compensation is not new. Johnita Scott, a member of the
National Coalition of Blacks for Reparations in America
(N'COBRA), covers the history of US reparations to African
Americans, from the never-fulfilled promise of forty acres and a
mule to the current welter of legislative and grassroots proposals.
Supporters of reparations are quick to note, and Ms. Scott underscores this point, that the demand is not merely for money, "a
check in the mail for 35 million descendants of the slaves." Repara-
tions activists want improved health care, better schools, drug
treatment programs, decent, affordable housing, the relief of
African debt, and targeted prevention and treatment programs for
African Americans and Africans with HIV/AIDS.

The challenges faced by African Americans with HIV/AIDS
are pressing concerns to activists like Phill Wilson, whose Califor-
nia-based African American AIDS Policy and Training Institute is
a leading advocacy organization. Wilson cites the grim statistics:
"In the United States, while Blacks represent around 12 percent of
the total US population, we account for 37.7 percent of the accumulated AIDS cases and over 50 percent of new AIDS cases. In
2000, Black men made up 40 percent of the new AIDS cases
among males, Black women represented 62 percent of reported
AIDS cases among females, and 6.2 out of every 10 children reported with AIDS in the US were Black." Wilson believes that
without increased awareness and dialogue, the epidemic will remain a national threat. If we want to decrease the rate of HIV infection among African Americans, he asserts, we need to increase
the dialogue—not shut it down. "For African American institutions, this means supporting visible gay Black leadership, and not

just assuming that antigay prejudice is someone else's problem. For individual Black men, it means expanding the way we think—not just about straight and gay, but about the whole range of human possibilities." Wilson argues that effective counseling, affordable vaccines, and other pharmaceutical drugs are also critical to reducing the spread of AIDS, and these elements are needed especially in Africa, where a pandemic is emerging.

There are only few countries in Africa where AIDS is not a major concern, but as Salih Booker points out, civil war is also devastating the continent. At the root of this Cairo-to-Capetown turmoil is the legacy of colonialism, Booker writes, and while the US may have been only a minor player in the past, its current grip, through a host of multinational corporations, has broad consequences. Whether in the area of reproductive health or the AIDS crisis, Booker sees the US as a chief culprit.

Symbolizing inadequate US policy in Africa are two African Americans who possess little or no understanding of African affairs according to Booker: "Neither Condoleezza Rice nor Secretary of State Colin Powell ... has demonstrated a particular interest in or special knowledge of Africa. Moreover, both Powell and Rice are loyal Republicans with a shared orientation toward international affairs that derives from a narrow, militaristic understanding of security. They are also unilateralists at a time when the need in Africa is for multilateral support for peace and security."

The failure of US policy in Africa is further borne out by the recent debacle in Zimbabwe during the presidential elections, Booker notes. And while the US remains far in arrears in its dues payments to the UN, it is highly unlikely that the current administration will accede to the wishes of activists demanding the cancellation of African debt to the US, the International Monetary Fund (IMF), or the World Bank.

Nor is there a concerted effort to do anything about the environmental hazards from carbon dioxide emissions. A number of experts have warned that Africa would suffer most from the effects of global warming. Like the AIDS pandemic that is wreaking havoc on African societies and economies, global warming is clearly taking a toll among poor countries in the South, mainly in Africa.

These consequences are not merely the result of 'natural' disasters compounded by neglect on the part of the richest country on earth. They are the strange fruit of what amounts to years of aggressive and irresponsible behavior by the US.

Toxic emissions, waste sites, and hazardous incinerators are not limited to Africa and other Third World countries. These threats to public health are known intimately in cities like Detroit. Charles Simmons is among a growing army of concerned citizens in the city working to reduce air pollution that makes breathing almost impossible for children with asthma. And, according to Simmons, heavy emission of pollutants may also be associated with the high incidence of various forms of cancer and lung disease. Before discussing the success of a local initiative, Simmons sums up the difference between the old and new environmentalists. "[T]raditional environmentalism has generally focused on the impact of pollution on wildlife, air, and water," he begins. "The environmental justice movement focuses on the hazardous impact of pollutants on the human habitat, especially the urban communities where people of color and poor and working-class folks live. And in many communities, the people who are responsible for children—parents, grandparents, and extended family members—are the activists who are leading environmental justice (EJ) campaigns. Motivated by concerns about the health of their children and grandchildren, these activists have deep roots in the community and churches, and are able to mobilize support and interest in their cause, often through personal connections. This grassroots movement also boasts civil rights activists and scholars with international reputations who are advocates. . ."

In Detroit, a campaign for environmental justice is well under way, and it could be a model for creating sustainable cities across the nation. "We need new ideas about how to develop our communities and cities, and the old top-down method of leadership has not worked for us. Let us encourage our youth to join in this struggle. They can work, learn, and grow while contributing to well-being of their the communities."

The writers, scholars and activists assembled here under the heading *Race and Resistance* are emblematic of the thousands who, with each passing day, take a more determined interest in ridding our world of debilitating hazards, be they toxic, sexist, homophobic, or racist. Many important issues—welfare, education, housing, and domestic violence, for example—are not covered as extensively here as we would have liked, but as you can see, to paraphrase the great African patriot Amilcar Cabral, we have told no lies, and claimed no easy victories.

We hope this collection will play a small part in generating the "possible world" that social justice activists have called for in progressive gatherings in Porto Alegre, Brazil; Durban, South Africa; and Washington, DC. As Phill Wilson writes, "we're the ones we've been waiting for."

Chapter 1

Racism

Looking Forward, Looking Back

Ron Daniels

This essay is based on a speech given to the Z Media Institute in June, 1996.

In terms of propositions, I want to lay out the following: Number one, that theories of race and attitudes of racial superiority and inferiority, prejudice and bigotry, evolved into an institutionalized system of discrimination, of exclusion, of deprivation, and oppression based on color or race—the accidental quality, if you will, of color/race. In the Black community, very often we call this a system of white supremacy or white domination.

Proposition two: Racism and cultural aggression were and are highly destructive of people of color in terms of the struggle to develop and sustain community and "peopleness." This is particularly true of native people in this country and African Americans, who have suffered the most extreme cases of the impact of racism and cultural aggression. Proposition three: Historically, racism constituted and constitutes a system of special privileges, benefits, and psychological and symbolic and material rewards for white people. Indeed, one might characterize the system as a long-standing affirmative action program for white people. Proposition number four: Historically, racism has been used and is used as a mechanism and a strategy to divide and exploit people of color and poor and working people, particularly to divide between white working class people and poor people and whites in general and people of color. Therefore, in this regard it retards the ability to organize along class lines. The final proposition is the thesis of this discussion: that the creation of a new society with genuine political and economic democracy is impossible without the eradication of institutional racism and the breakup of white supremacy.

In talking about racism we need to have some sense of definitions. I want to present definitions at this point. Racism is not defined by individual random acts. Racism is a systematic discrimination against or exclusion and oppression of a group of people based upon an accidental quality such as skin color, hair texture, shape and size of lips, and so forth. It's systematic. Racism is to be distinguished from chauvinism. Much of what we often call racism is really not racism at all, but may be cultural or ethnic chauvinism. And chauvinism is often an attitude of superiority based on culture or ethnicity. One group of people feels that their cultural group is superior to another, or one ethnic group may feel that it is better than another group. Then there's prejudice. Prejudice is simply a feeling of superiority or bias towards a group of people. Generally, we talk about prejudice in terms of the pre-judging of people.

But racism is much more than chauvinism or prejudice. I could stand here and say that I think, culturally or ethnically, I'm better. I may have certain prejudices. And certainly we all do. But racism is distinguished by the fact that it is systemic and it relates to the question of power and capacity. That is to say, racism is about having the power or capacity to translate prejudices and attitudes or feelings of superiority into practice, custom, policy, or law. That is a fundamental difference between simply saying "I don't like white folks," or, "I don't like Black folks," and the ability to impose that prejudice in a way that impinges upon and thwarts the ability of a group to develop. But it becomes very alarming when they have the power, through various institutions and mechanisms, to translate that dislike into policies and customs that block me and impede my ability to fulfill myself as a human being, or even to do violence to my person.

In that regard, some of the terms that have come into prominent usage—particularly on the right, with the advent of

Reaganism, Bush, and the right wing—such terms as "reverse discrimination," which may be possible, or "Black racism," which is almost an oxymoron. Can Black people be racist? Yes, but it implies being in circumstances and situations where there is the capacity to take antiwhite attitudes and to translate them into systems that thwart and impede the ability of white people to develop. Quite frankly, that has not been the history here in the US. That does not mean that you don't have Black people who are prejudiced, who are bigoted, who get up and say bigoted things. But that is not in my judgment to be confused with racism. In fact, in some ways, to do that is to belittle the travail of slavery, the long history of racism and racist violence that has afflicted African people in this country.

What I'd like to do is spend a minute on the history of racism. Some of us believe that racism always existed, that this was something that was deeply embedded in the American character, something that we had little opportunity to do anything about. In reality, race theory and racism are relatively recent developments in world history. If one were to go back and read the ancients— Herodotus, the Greeks and others—what one would find in the ancient world is cultural chauvinism. The Greeks felt that they had the best civilization going. The Romans felt likewise. And there was prejudice and chauvinism. People fought each other based on that. But it was not on the basis of skin color, by and large. In fact, we are hard-pressed to find it on the basis of skin color. Indeed, among the Greeks there were leading African people. Among the Romans there were leading African people, some of whom became Roman emperors. As Roman emperors, they thought they were better than anybody else, including other Black people who were non-Roman. So discrimination and conflicts between groups were not about race, not about color. It was more about culture. It was more about a sense of cultural superiority or chauvinism than it was about skin color. In fact, Herodotus and some of the others who wrote about the ancient world talked about the virtues of Black people, about Ethiopia being a place in Africa that was highly civilized. So we have to look elsewhere for the origins of racism as a systematic theory than in the ancient world.

Where we find the origins of racism, in terms of race theory and its practice, is in association with the transatlantic slave trade. In some respects, it was an outgrowth of the transatlantic slave trade. It emerged as a rationale and justification for the massive human carnage that has come to be called the "African holocaust," in which by some estimates 100 million Africans may have lost their lives. So you had people like Gobineau, the French philosopher/theorist, beginning to come up with these notions that there are races and that races have different characteristics and that there's a continuum from racial superiority to racial inferiority. That the Indo-Aryan or Caucasian is the superior and there are some people who are yellow who are not quite as good as the white folks but still better than others, and then brown and black and whatever. That became the continuum of superiority to inferiority. One of the most important points to stress is that black is the defining color. It is black/white. And even though there are other levels of discrimination involved, the defining color in terms of inferiority is black. The defining color in terms of superiority is white. So in the Black community they have this phrase that sort of captures it: If you're white you're all right. Yellow, mellow. Brown, stick around. Black, get back. In that sense, when you look at the history of how this has played out—and it's still playing out—Black people are always at the bottom of the ladder in terms of racial discrimination. In societies like South Africa, where there is miscegenation and you have the "coloreds," the coloreds will be seen as being a notch or two above the Blacks because their skin color is lighter. Even inside some African communities, those who are seen as high yellow, or "light, bright, and damn near white," as we used to say in the Black community, are given more privileges.

When the civil rights movement first erupted in the North and we in Northern communities were in sympathy strikes and sympathy demonstrations with those in the South, it was interesting to see people begin to hire Black people and put Black people visibly up front. The first people they hired were always the very, very, very lightest Black people. Because there's a sense that the darker you are, the more inferior you are. So black is the defining color. That becomes important because there is often, in this country and in the world, manipulation between peoples of color based on skin color. If one is from another background, other than African, and light, very often the system will give one advantages and rewards that not quite the same as those reserved for white people, but are certainly more than one would get if one were Black. This has to be considered when laying out the whole schematic of racism.

I also want to introduce another aspect of this discussion that is very seldom touched upon but is nevertheless another insidious dimension of the oppression of Black people and particularly indigenous people in this society. It is "cultural aggression," by which we mean the effort to take away culture or to substitute the so-called "dominant" culture for the culture of the subject people. Native people and African people were often asked to adopt or to internalize the culture of the colonizer or the oppressor. For example, there was a concerted drive to have Christian and European education for indigenous people, to teach them to view their indigenous-ness or their Native American-ness or their Indian-ness as being negative. Therefore, they had to become Christianized, including Christianizing their names as a way of "becoming human" and being accepted. This whole question of cultural aggression is another devastating aspect of the oppression of African people in this country. It's one that we need to understand if we are to be able to look at the evolutionary development of the African American community or the retardation of the African American community. To some extent, racism and racial prejudice are fueled by a lack of understanding of how the African community developed. For example, people say, "If my forebears could come over here and make it, what is wrong with Black people? Why are they still in such a bad condition?"

One of the things that has to be taken into account in answering such questions is the issue of cultural aggression. In terms of cultural aggression, particularly in the slave experience, African slaves were taught that their color was a badge of degradation, that their culture was a mark of inferiority, that it tainted them. There was the question of cultural disruption. If culture is the stuff that makes a people stick together, and I argue that it is, that culture is the accumulated experiences of a people, and if you attack it, then of course people become unstuck. It becomes very problematic to maintain group cohesion and group togetherness. In the case of Africans in North America in particular, the African experience was the most brutal and devastating at the level of culture. Slavery was very bad in the Caribbean, and in Central and South America, but only in North America was there a British-American chattel form of slavery where the African was reduced to property. Total dehumanization. In addition to that, there was a system for making sure that not too many people of the same ethnic group populated the same plantation. There was a conscious policy of dispersion. That is to say, they didn't want too many Yorubas or Hausas to be on the same plantation. Why? Because if they were there and they could communicate, they could then more readily engage in slave revolts. So there was a policy of spreading them out.

But not only that. African slaves were forbidden to practice their religion, to speak their language, to play their musical instruments. At the level of cultural aggression, there was an effort to de-Africanize the African, to make the African something other. This was again very devastating because it meant striking at the heart of those institutions and those dimensions that hold a people together. It's like more recent efforts to Europeanize the Native Americans, but also the effort to impose English-only education and to impose European culture on Latinos.

Another aspect of cultural aggression has to do with the fact of being Black in a predominantly white society, the fact of being Black in a cultural framework where white is always glorified and where black is always denigrated. That's another dimension of the struggle to survive and develop within the context of America. There is racism, but there are also other external/internal forces which retard the development of the Black community. There's this white vs. black image in symbols. In English literature, for example, black is almost always seen as evil. The dominant tendency is seen in expressions like the "black sheep" of the family. Behind the eight ball. Black market. Blackball. Blacklist. Blackmail. I was in a church one Sunday, and the pastor wanted to talk about sin real bad. He used the adjective "black" to indicate the worst: "It is a black sin." A dark day in history. Black Monday at the stock market. You see what I'm saying? There is that constant reference to black as negative. In the movies: Darth Vader. There was a movie with Sylvester Stallone and Wesley Snipes in it. Stallone was the greatest cop of all time and Snipes—I don't understand how he even allowed himself to play this role—the greatest criminal of all time. So here you had white Stallone and Black Snipes in the traditional imagery of white is good and black is evil. You begin to internalize. There's no question. Racism is internalizing one's sense of inferiority based on these kinds of images, and it's a very devastating kind of thing. A black lie is very bad, but if you tell a little white lie, it's okay. Or it's like angel's food cake and devil's food cake.

European immigrants did not go through the same experience. It is important to answer the question, Why have European immigrants been able to move forward more rapidly? They came with language intact, religion intact. The European immigrants were able to set up the Little Italies and Little Polands, and couched in there were little subeconomies based on culture. Of course they were white, so even if you wanted to discriminate against them on the basis of their Italian-ness or their Irish-ness, you really couldn't do it. There was a time in American history when that was tried. The Southern Europeans, the Italians, the Greeks, and the Eastern Europeans were considered not quite up to snuff. They were seen as being a little darker, because we've got to keep this racist thing going, and they were from the global South. Many of them were Catholic, which wasn't too good in this white, Anglo-Saxon, Protestant nation. You might still have to guess. But you don't have to guess about blood. It's usually very obvious who Black people are. So there was a vast difference in the experience, not the least of which was cultural continuity. The Europeans came with their culture intact, and that culture could serve as a basis of integration, assimilation, or incorporation into the American body politic and the American social and economic political system much more readily than has been true of Africans. So I just wanted to express that so people hopefully have a more profound understanding of that aspect of the Black experience within the broader question of racism and some of its ancillary and associated impacts.

Now what I want to do is turn to this issue of racism as an affirmative action program for white people.

First of all, let me suggest that to the extent that there was ever anything in American society that was white only, it was a system of exclusive benefits for a particular group. White only is like having a set-aside program for white people. Certain jobs, certain things were set aside and only white people could benefit from them. So therefore there's a question of power, of rewards. Consequently, it pays to be white because it translates into the fact that white people are the first hired and the last fired. Black people are the last hired and the first to be fired. So there is a benefit, a material benefit. Does that benefit accrue to all white people equally? It certainly does not, because there's a class dimension within capitalist society. Those white people near the top benefit more. But it still, relatively speaking, pays to be white vis-à-vis being Black in American society.

Beyond that, there is the question of intergenerational benefits and intergenerational deficits. If at a particular period in time, Black people or women or any particular group are excluded from work or from any aspect of opportunity, then the accumulated benefits that result just don't stay in a particular period of time. They are passed on intergenerationally. That is to say, privilege becomes a benefit that is passed on. Therefore, if you are able, at a particular point, to get the job because your father got the job, and my father could not get the job in the context of a then largely male-dominated society, it would mean that those benefits could be passed on. It was a benefit to your line; it was a deficit, a handicap to my line. So to talk about affirmative action in the sense of saying, "Let's abolish it, let's suddenly be color-blind, just wipe it all out and everybody starts even," is nonsense. You're not starting just even. It's like starting a race and one group of people are starting with balls and chains around their legs and about halfway through the race somebody says, "Wait a minute. I think we should have an equal race. So let's cut the ball and chain off the people's legs." By that time, somebody's at the 200-yard line, and I'm still struggling to get to the 40-yard line. So it really doesn't quite work out. There's got to be a way of compensating for the kind of intergenerational benefits and deficits that have accrued based on this kind of racism, this kind of affirmative action for white people, the set-asides and all those things that come through them.

To illustrate this in a more concrete way, and to combine points here, I want to talk a little bit about the whole strategy of racism as a system of dividing and exploiting, particularly in terms of driving divisions within the working class. In order to do that, I want to use several quick illustrations and focus heavily on the post-Reconstruction period.

In terms of racism as a strategy of divide-and-exploit, if one goes back historically to slavery times, very often in the South slave masters would hire out their slaves to enterprises, to small businesses in the urban areas. The result of that was that this slave labor, which was hired out at very, very cheap wages, undercut free labor. The problem is that the white folks who found themselves victimized by the system could never quite get the point that it was not the slaves who were the villains, that they were in fact being manipulated also. So the venom always tended to be aimed at the slaves rather than at the collusion between the white businesspeople and the white slave masters. That's been a historical phenomenon. People are deflected away from the real manipulators, the real villains. This was also true about the system called the convict lease system. After the Civil War, large numbers of people were freed but freed to do what? They didn't have jobs, land, property. So vagrancy laws were passed.

One of the things I often challenge my African American brothers and sisters on, when we get a little beside ourselves and start talking about Europeans and how this country was peopled by criminals is to point out that in a certain sense, it's the same thing. When you had the policy of the enclosures in Europe, in England in particular, people were thrown off the land and went into the cities by the thousands. They had nothing to do, no jobs, and they were not immediately absorbed. England passed vagrancy laws and all kind of laws against paupers. As a result, many of them ended up being criminalized and arrested. Those are the criminals we're talking about. They weren't really hard criminals. They were people who had been criminalized. So we have to be careful when we talk about this country being populated by criminals. They were people who had been criminalized.

Similarly, this was the situation after the Civil War. Some of the people who went into the convict lease system were poor white people, but they were overwhelmingly Black. What happened is, the prison system would often lease out convicts to do work for companies in the community. Of course, it had the same effect as slavery: It undercut free white labor. It created a great deal of animosity, though in this instance, I must say, there were some times, when white labor did rise up and fight against the convict lease system. Everyone should be familiar with the history of strike breaking. Very often Blacks were used to break strikes when the labor movement was organizing. Again, it's easy to become angry at the Blacks who were being used in this way. In fact, what was happening again was the manipulation of Blacks by the bosses. Not enough anger was directed against the bosses, but a hell of a lot of antipathy was turned towards Black people, part of which had to do, again, with the question of racism.

I want to focus on the post-Reconstruction period because I think this period is very illustrative of some of the things that are going on today. It also clarifies some of the points that I'm trying to make around the affirmative action issue. After the Civil War, there was a period called "radical reconstruction" or "Black reconstruction." It was called radical reconstruction because of the passage of the Thirteenth, Fourteenth, and Fifteenth Amendments, as well as two other little-known acts, the Civil Rights Acts of 1868 and 1875. In Black or radical reconstruction, Black people had more political power than any other time, including the present. There were Black elected officials, Black legislators who acquitted themselves well and passed a lot of very progressive legislation. There were some problems, but by and large for a people inexperienced in governance, they did an incredible job. They were, however, governing at the behest of the Republican Party, who sold Black people out in 1876–77. I won't go into all the details of it. In 1877, all the federal troops were pulled out of the South and the plight of the so-called Negro was turned over to the so-called redeemers in the South, a new, emerging, white power elite.

One of the pledges that these redeemers made was that they would not brutalize Black people, and they indicated that they preferred to associate with the better class of Negroes than with what they themselves called "white trash." The problem is that something happened in the South. There was not the immediate imposition of Southern apartheid, the Jim Crow system that we fought to overturn in the civil rights revolution of the 1960s and 1970s. For a while after 1877, the first three or four years, everything was sort of okay. Black people continued to vote, to be on public conveyances. Things were different, but not radically so.

But there was a development. In one of the most rare moments in the South, you had a development where large numbers of white farmers and white workers formed the Populist movement. In that movement they were demanding economic justice. They were opposed to and angry at policies that were being passed which they saw as being antithetical and oppressive to their interests. The rarity is that they also reached out to a large movement of Black farmers and Black workers, particularly the farmers who were organized into Negro farmer alliances by the thousands. They reached out to them. They joined hands in this movement and they came dangerously close, from the perspective of the ruling class in the South, to overturning the system through the electoral process. They were winning some seats. They came very, very close. This set off an alarm in an elite that previously wasn't too concerned about Black people. They made a decision that never again would this alliance of Blacks and whites threaten the interests of the power structure in the South. It was only at that point that they instituted the system of Southern apartheid. They did it by appealing to racism, to race. They said to their white kith and kin, Come on, now. This is an argument among white people here. Why do we have niggers involved in this? We can settle this. We should not have Black people interfering in white folks' business. So we can work this out. Unfortunately, the white Populist movement and its leadership fell for this. There were a number of things that were done to reinforce this split, this division among working class people. You have then Jim Crow. You had the psychological incentives. It paid to be white. You could have your own water fountains, just for white people. When you had to go into certain essential functions, like going to the jane or john, you'd have your own bathroom. After all, imagine the indignity of having to sit down and take care of this essential business with a darkie, a jungle bunny, next door.

So white people were given their own bathrooms, their own water fountains. You didn't have to ride on public conveyances with niggers any more. These uncivilized jungle bunnies, darkies. Indeed, even when you died, you'd be able to have death in dignity. You had your own cemetery. The niggers will have theirs over there, and everything will be just fine. But it went further than that. Those were the psychological incentives of being white, by having these special privileges. But they added material incentives as well, which went like this: There would be certain jobs that only white people could work. We will set aside—I use that term advisedly— certain jobs that only white people will be allowed to work. And if there are jobs where Black people and white people have to work the same jobs, then white people will always be paid more, considerably more, for working those jobs than Black people. So what you had was a system of psychological and material incentives to drive a wedge between Blacks and whites.

The fact of the matter is, both Blacks and whites were being exploited by the big white man. The big white boss was exploiting Blacks and whites. Blacks were being exploited more, but the poor whites were only slightly better off, actually, having these material and psychological incentives. The real deal is, these cats were getting off like bandits all the way to the bank with the loot that they were expropriating—if I'm allowed to used that term—from the labor of both Black and white. The point is that this wedge was driven. Racism was and is a strategy of dividing and exploiting working people. That has been, unfortunately, a deep and embedded part of American history that we are forced today to try to overcome.

As a quick aside, we did have the Knights of Labor, which had a strong program of racial inclusion, the Longshoremen's Union, the Wobblies, any number of other groups who did an excellent job of including Black people in their ranks in terms of fighting for labor rights and for economic and social justice.

I want to come back just for a minute to those set-aside programs. Not only to look at them from the North, but to make the point that while this was a Jim Crow system in the South, it was also a Jim Crow system in the North. Black people moved to the North because there was a promise of better jobs. And they got better jobs. Another sidebar is, Black people unfortunately were held in the South as slaves, wage slaves, sharecroppers, agricultural laborers, and tenant farmers after the Civil War. One of the things that those of us who talk about reparations deal with is that we had political rights—we were made citizens—but we did not have social rights. We were not given land and capital within a capitalist society. It's very difficult to compete. So Black people would have loved to come to the North earlier. But one of the things that happened is that there was a conscious collusion between Northern industrialists and the power structure in the South to keep Black people in the South, keep them working in these low-paying jobs, or sharecropping. Because cotton still remained king for a long period of time after the Civil War. What happened is, therefore, the demand for labor that went with a growing capitalist economy in the North, Northeast, and Midwest was filled not by Black people, who would have loved to have these jobs in the industrial sector, but by millions of European immigrants who came across the Atlantic.

Here's what I want you to look at: Even though we had to struggle to get better working conditions in the labor movement for white workers or workers in general because people were being paid a low wage, working in a factory or a mine or a steel mill was a hell of a lot better and paid a hell of a lot more even at the lowest level than being a sharecropper. In other words, if Black people could have moved North and taken those jobs, they would have been better off economically. But instead they were held in the South. Other people came in, took those jobs, and therefore had a step up in economic terms on those who had been locked in the South. When Black people did come North, they ran into the same system. My father worked in the steel mills. In my lifetime I remember jobs that Black people could not have. They could not work in the upper echelons in the steel mills. They were frozen out of those jobs in Cleveland, Ohio, in Pittsburgh, in Youngstown,

Ohio. The point is, there was this system of affirmative action for white people in which the benefits accrued intergenerationally to people who now are better-positioned in American society because of these racial set-asides and this affirmative action program. Therefore, affirmative action for people of color, while not perfect, is a remedy that we need to look at and fight for.

Having made the point about racism as a system of divide-and-exploit, let me now turn to more contemporary history. For example, the critical subtext of Reaganism and Reaganomics was race. It was another effort to divide and exploit that worked extremely well. Ronald Reagan was a B movie actor. He never got an Academy Award or nomination, but he deserves the Academy Award of the century as president of the US because he fooled a hell of a lot of people with his performance as president. He persuaded the American people at a time of crisis, of stagflation and insecurity, that the burden of government had to be lifted off the backs of the American people. Translation: All of those Black people and people of color who are on welfare, food stamps, all these social programs, and burgeoning entitlements are really the cause of the crisis in American society in terms of jobs and insecurity. What he did was a massive scapegoating job: welfare, food stamps, social programs. He focused on the ghettos, the barrios, the reservations. This was the burden on government. Therefore enact crippling cuts, transfer payments, increase the military budget. He didn't cut the budget. He transferred money to the military budget. He transferred money to the rich and the super-rich, loosened up the regulations on banking and savings and loans and any number of other things. He helped to produce one of the greatest scandals in American history, the Savings and Loan (S&L) scandal. It's very interesting, because there were no welfare mothers or homeless people involved in the S&L scandal. We're talking about modifying the behavior of welfare mothers and making them more responsible and accountable. What about $600 million or a billion dollars over 30 years? What about that? And not having these so-called "reckless" people involved in it?

The civil rights movement and all of the social movements of the sixties really benefitted as many white people as Black people.

In fact, they benefitted more white people. This movement that emanated out of the Black community did not take rights away from white people. It guaranteed more rights. Social and economic rights. Because there are more white people on welfare than Black people. There are more white people on virtually every one of these programs than Black people. Black people may be disproportionately on these programs on the basis of their condition, but they have also serviced in a very admirable way large numbers of people. And yet, we have white people who really believe that Black welfare recipients get more than they get. There are white people who really believe that Black people get more benefits. In these church burnings where they're trying to say there's no linkage, in one of the incidents, the people who were arrested said they attacked Black churches because in the Black church they were teaching people how to get on welfare. There is this sense of welfare as a burden on the back of people.

So what we see here is this diversion. During the Reagan Administration, we know that the white rich got richer. White men got richer. And the poor got poorer. And yet that was not the focus. People don't talk about the S&L scandal. They don't talk about the HUD (Housing and Urban Development) scandal. They don't talk about the FDIC. They don't talk about the obscene fortunes. Michael Milken, how much did he make? He paid back $600 or $700 million. He still was able to keep about half a billion dollars. Obscene fortunes were being made, as Jesse Jackson talked about merging, purging, and submerging the US economy. And yet people were angry at Black people and people of color, as opposed to being angry at corporations, the rich, and the super-rich. Another instance of dividing and exploiting and a digression away from the real issues, the real contradictions, the real victimizers.

Having blinders, racial blinders. Joe Sixpack, pissed off and angry because things are going bad, but never realizing that he is victimized by corporations and by the agenda of the radical right. In fact, one of the anomalies of the 1980s is that 40 percent of labor voted for Ronald Reagan. Even today, regarding the agenda of the radical right, one asks, how could it be sustained by the majority of the American people, or even the majority of those who vote in this election and who voted in the election of 1994 if it is in fact against Medicaid, against Social Security, against the whole culture of rights we see reflected in the New Deal that benefit not just Black people but the American people in general, how could that happen? It could only happen, in my opinion, because racism is the critical subtext for policy in this country.

Remember Willie Horton? What has happened in this country is that people are playing politics, racial politics. They're playing the race card as a way of dividing and exploiting. Meanwhile, America has the greatest inequality of any Western democracy, according to a report in *Z Magazine*.

I'm not going to give a litany of all the crises in communities of color. They are very deep. Suffice it to say that there is a serious avoidance of debate and discussion about racism in American society. One recalls when Lani Guinier was chumped off by her dear friend Clinton, he said in part that he did not want to see a divisive debate on race in American society. It's not just a matter of past racism. It's a matter of ongoing racism. In one out of five instances in American society where Black people who have exactly the same qualifications as their white counterparts go to the bank to get a mortgage, they are denied. This also applies to franchises and places like Denny's, where Black people were insulted very recently. Racism is rampant in American society. There are instances now where Black people are being chased out of white neighborhoods.

More importantly, at the institutional level there is the question of urban policy. There is no urban policy. There is no plan to deal with resuscitating inner-city education. As Richard Moore of the Southwest Organizing Committee said, "We are the wrong complexion to get the protection."

What do we do about it? There are several points I want to stress. One, it seems to me that many people support the issue of multicultural education. Multicultural education and diversity training are important. It's imperative to dispel myths and lies and misinformation because in so doing we undermine the pillars of white supremacy. A lot of this is simply predicated on misinformation. There's a book by Carter G. Woodson called *The Miseducation of the Negro.* I submit that the same proposition applies to most of the American population. We are miseducated. We know very little about Latino history, very little about indigenous history, very little about African American history. What if Howard Zinn's *A People's History of the United States* was a standard textbook? It would impact the way we see the world. We would see the whole world differently. We're struggling now with feminist studies, lesbian and gay studies. All of these things are designed to break up this white male hegemony. That's what the Contract on America was in reaction to, that's what it was all about. There is a perception in this country that it's a white country, that if you accommodate to this white, Anglo-Saxon, Protestant milieu culturally and politically, it's fine. But if you challenge it, that's cause for deep fear, deep anxiety. And some of this lashing out is about that. But we have to relax and deal with it.

We must wage a relentless struggle to ban discrimination in all of its forms. We cannot relax on that struggle. To enforce all civil rights laws in the search for meaningful remedies to heal the damages of racism and cultural aggression. That includes the awarding of reparations, which is not popular, but nonetheless essential, I think. The goal of the society is not so much integration and assimilation, at least from the vantage point of most African Americans. It is a question of equity and parity. The ability to gain access to American society and to be equal and on par with other groups within American society. We need to fight to end the underdevelopment. Manning Marable wrote a book called *How Capitalism Underdeveloped Black America.* We need to talk about how to end that underdevelopment.

We need to talk about corporate and individual responsibility and accountability in terms of programs that could focus on helping to remedy this condition of underdevelopment. We need a concerted, scientific, and systematic program to fight racism in the white community, particularly among poor and working people and the middle class. We can't afford to not work on racist attitudes in white communities. This is a major challenge that I've been dwelling on now for many years. Whites often ask about the question of organizing in communities of color. I would say, Yes, there's nothing wrong with that. But there's a priority of working and organizing against racism in white communities. Antiracism campaigns in white communities. If one chooses to work with, not in but with, communities of color, the goal must always be organizing with communities of color to empower those communities and for them to more effectively lead themselves around an agenda that they see as essential and important.

In many respects we have to struggle against not only racism but paternalism, the whole notion that somehow these people are just not able. There's a great fear in the Black community that people who come in from the outside really want to get off their jones and lead in the Black community, as opposed to enabling and empowering and supporting the movements in that particular community.

There are some guidelines that one should take into account in this regard. We should always respect the culture and identity of communities of color. Respect the leadership and agenda of peoples of color. Serve as a facilitator, not the leader. The facilitator, the enable, the supporter, as opposed to the leader. Predominantly white organizations should always have people of color in critical roles on their staff so they can take the lead in organizing in communities of color. This doesn't mean that only white people can organize in white communities, or Black people in Black communities. There are some priorities that we're speaking about here. We could have interracial teams doing work, and we certainly need interracial collaboration on strategies to move this work forward. Certainly Black people and people of color need to take the lead in organizing in their own communities.

People of color caucuses are also important within predominantly white structures. People should not see them in a frightening kind of way. They should not be fearful of people of color caucuses. Indeed, they often have women's caucuses and lesbian and gay caucuses within structures. So these are some very brief guidelines.

There also is a need for joint work. In fact, we cannot do this simply by seeing the Klan show up and throwing rocks and bricks at them and cursing at them profusely. That is simply not going to solve the problem. That's sometimes our definition of antiracism work. We get out, the Klan shows up, all seven of them, 300 of us show up, throw rocks at them, call them bad names. We go home and we've done our work for the year. We need some real serious, joint work based on mutually acceptable agendas of issues. One of the areas I'm very keen on is environmental justice, fighting against environmental racism, environmental deprivation, and uniting in the struggle for environmental justice. It is a common-ground issue that deals with things like housing and health and community development. All those issues are encapsulated in environmental justice.

We must recognize the centrality of the agendas and leadership in communities of color in the struggle to create a new society. I happen to believe that those who have been most victimized by the systems of society must be in the forefront, must be in the lead, not only in terms of rescuing themselves. As I look at the recent wave of church burnings, I believe that Black people should seize this opportunity and talk about the broader sets of issues, to use it as an opportunity to emerge as the moral conscience of the nation. In that regard, this violence is not just about Black people. It's about all oppressed people.

We're not really fighting against racism so we can have better race relations. So we can all sit down and have tea together. That's fine, but not within the context of an exploitive society. The real challenge, our real mission is to fundamentally transform this capitalist political economy. To create nonoppressive structures, to create structures that are human-centered, that are earth-centered, which means that there is a fundamental transformation which must take place. To have that we must have racial justice, not just good race relations. Racial justice is an indispensable prerequisite to the overall struggle for a better society, as is gender equality and rights for lesbian and gay people and the eradication of religious bigotry. All of these things become critical cornerstones to the new society which we must forge and which we must build. I happen to think that the struggle against racism, as DuBois said, the problem of the color line, the color barrier, will be the barrier of the twentieth century and may well be into the twenty-first century.

So I close this meditation on racism by simply saying that to talk about fighting against racism is to talk about revolution. We need to struggle against racism so that we can in fact create a force that will be at the cutting edge of the fight for social transformation and the creation of a new society and a new world. Nothing else really makes sense. It's not really an academic discussion. It's not an academic exercise. This is a real-life discussion about what's going on right now, the threats that it poses. In many respects, 1996 looked like 1896, not only in terms of the turning back of the clock on Black progress. If you understood what I had to say about the whole divide-and-exploit strategy in the post-Reconstruction period, this is also a period in which racism is thwarting the development of average poor white and working people in the middle class, not permitting them to fulfill their aspirations. Because they are blinded to the realities and the contradictions of the accumulation of wealth and power in the hands of the few. If we are to unite the many to defeat the few—and we must—then the struggle against racism is indispensable. We cannot really achieve a society based on genuine economic and political democracy unless we win that fight. And brothers and sisters and friends, I know that we will.

Chapter 2

Still at the Periphery

The Economic Status of African Americans

Julianne Malveaux

Whether you measure income, wealth, home ownership, or employment status, the differences in economic status between African Americans and whites are significant and persistent. To be sure, some gaps are narrowing. African Americans have vastly improved their status since 1940, when more than half of us lived in poverty, and 70 percent of all African American women worked as private household workers. Visible indicators of success include magazine covers touting the presence of African Americans in management (see, for example, *Newsweek,* January 20, 2002). But the status of African Americans in the middle and at the bottom is far less visible, and far more often ignored.

Average data paints a good comparative picture. According to the 2000 census, mean white wage and salary income was $36,249, compared to $25,960 for African Americans. Thus, African Americans earned 71.6 percent of what whites earned. While education and occupational choices are factors, there is an earning gap between whites and people of color even when we control for education. For example, among men over age 25 with a bachelor's degree or more, African Americans earned $40,360, and white men earned $51,469. In percentage terms, college-educated African American men earned 78 percent of what white men earned.[1]

Yet, income data provides an incomplete picture of the economic status of African Americans. The long-term status of African Americans is better reflected by wealth data, and here the gaps are more glaring. The Survey of Consumer Finance,[2] which reports on wealth status every three years, aggregates African Americans and Hispanics in the category "nonwhite." In 1998, the latest year for which data is available,[3] the mean, or average, wealth for white families was $334,400, while the mean wealth for nonwhite families was $101,700. In other words, nonwhite families had just 30 percent of the wealth of white families.

Mean data perhaps present a more optimistic picture than the reality. Median wealth, or the level of wealth at which half of a population falls above and half falls below, in 1998 was $94,900 for white families and $16,400 for nonwhite families. The median wealth for nonwhite families was 17.2 percent of the wealth of white families. Interestingly, the median wealth of nonwhite families dropped by $400 between 1995 and 1998, while the median wealth of white families rose by more than $13,000, or 16%. During a period of economic expansion, then, nonwhite families at the bottom saw their wealth status erode.

One of the most important assets for middle-income people is a home. Indeed, home ownership is often the bridge over which low-income people cross to middle class status. Home ownership provides people with stability, but also with a vehicle to increase their net worth. The glaring racial gap in home ownership speaks to the many ways that economic expansion has had a limited reach. While overall home ownership in our nation reached an all-time high of 66.8 percent in 1999, the racial gap in home ownership narrowed only slightly amidst all this growth. Thus, while the rate of home ownership among whites grew to 73 percent, the rates remained at 46 and 45 percent, respectively, for African Americans and Hispanics. Home ownership among Asian Americans was about 54 percent, and it did not grow as much as the white rate grew during expansion.

Stagnant home ownership rates among people of color illustrate the limits of celebrating macroeconomic growth without looking at its microeconomic reverberations. Lower interest rates made it possible for more whites to own homes; it also increased their wealth basis, because refinancing allowed them to capitalize on the increased value of their homes. People of color who were in the same position had many of the same opportunities, but the large gap in home ownership statistics suggests that a sizable part of the African American and Hispanic population saw a market improve but had no opportunity to take advantage of it. Many were not home owners and could not buy, despite some examination of access to home ownership. Because they did not own homes, they could not engage in the kind of wealth accumulation that home owners, buoyed by interest rates that were lower than they have been in a generation (as low as six percent), were able to engage in.

The Impact of the "Boom Years"

Much has been made of the economic expansion that began in 1991 and continued for ten full years. During this expansion, gross domestic product grew by about four percent a year, and by as much as seven percent in some quarters. This expansion fueled a phenomenal growth in stock prices, with the Dow Jones Industrial average growing by more than 20 percent each year between 1995 and 1999. It also had a positive effect on the growth and development of small business, on the increased collection of federal, state, and local tax revenue, and on macroeconomic optimism. Unfortunately, though, while there was such macroeconomic ecstasy that Federal Reserve Board Chairman Alan Greenspan described the stock market as "irrationally exuberant," there was a persistent microeconomic angst because good times did not trickle down swiftly enough to people who lived at the periphery of the economy.

For many, then, living in the latter part of the twentieth century was like living in the midst of a party that one hadn't been invited to. It was like putting your nose up against the window of a candy store, watching others buy the brightly colored sweets while understanding that you had not the means to afford them. It was hearing about letting the good times roll, and being made to feel guilty because you weren't rolling with the good times. Indeed, between welfare deform and economic expansion, poverty was demonized. Once we believed that people who were poor were victims of an unjust system. By the late 1990s, the era of "no excuses," we began to believe that people were poor because there was something wrong with them.

So we raised the minimum wage in 1996, during an election year, and with much ado. But the minimum wage has not gone up since then, and more than 10 million Americans, mostly women, disproportionately women of color, and many mothers and household heads, earn just $10,700 a year when they work full-time, full year. The people who hold these jobs are essential to holding our worlds together—they care for our parents and our children, serve our food, and clean our hospitals. Yet they are disregarded, and are perhaps the sole group of people who can say they gained little or nothing from economic expansion. They have become a political pawn, ignored in the 2000 budget deliberations, held hostage to a set of business tax cuts in 2001 discussions. A disproportionate number of these workers are African American women.

They have jobs. The traditional ratio between Black and white unemployment, two to one, did not weaken during economic expansion and is debilitating during economic downturns. When the overall unemployment rate hovered at 4 percent, the white unemployment rate dipped to 3.5 percent and the Black unemployment rate was more than double, at 7.2 percent. In late 2001, with recession and the aftermath of September 11 driving layoffs, the overall unemployment rate in December was 5.8 percent, the white unemployment rate was 5.1 percent, and the Black unemployment rate was 10.2 percent, according to the Census Bureau's Current Population Survey. If a 10.2 percent unemployment rate were observed among the overall population, it would be interpreted as a "depression level" unemployment rate. Nevertheless, President George Bush has announced that he will cut funding for urban (read inner-city residents, mostly African American and Latino) job training programs by 70 percent, from $225 million to $45 million.

Thus, while some African Americans experienced benefits due to economic expansion, those at the bottom—the 25 percent who remain in poverty—did not find their circumstances much improved. Instead, thanks to "welfare deform," the demonization of poverty, and the blind eye that policymakers have turned to the poor their situation has actually gotten worse. Some few policy initiatives have focused on economic development and closing gaps, but the peripheral status of workers on the bottom, a disproportionate number of whom are African American, has been largely ignored.

Recession for Some, Depression for Others

If this was the case during expansion, it has been exacerbated during the economic contraction that began, according to the National Bureau of Economic Research, in March 2001, and is projected to continue through the third quarter of 2002. Those at the bottom are hit hardest, but even those who are not among the working poor can expect economic challenges. Many workers bounce back quickly from layoffs, but it often takes African American workers longer to find comparable jobs. The old saying of "last hired, first fired" for people of color has not been swept away by the new economy.

Beyond that, the economic slowdown means those corporations that briefly used their profits to engage inner-city residents in the new economy are now less likely to spend that money. Though no company has pulled its dollars out of programs to develop computer literacy, to train inner-city workers, or to wire inner-city community centers and churches for the Internet, companies who make contributions out of corporate profits now have much less to give. Those philanthropists who were awash in stock-market profits a year or two ago are now trying to make charitable dollars stretch, and they have less money to use for innovative programs.

Most corporations didn't do what they should have while the good times were rolling. Although some were energized by President Clinton's "emerging markets" initiative to boost development in inner cities and rural areas, that effort was too little, too late. The optimism that accompanied Clinton's 1999 trip through Appalachia, an Indian reservation, and several inner cities may be a faint memory if the economy doesn't turn around.

The slowdown has convinced many Democratic members of Congress and the Senate to at least partly support Bush's tax cuts, both those proposed in March 2001, and those that are part of

2003 budgeting. They say the economy needs stimulation and seem to think alternative minimum tax repeals and sops to the wealthy will do it. But those with average incomes won't get much, and African American median incomes are lower than average.

The "War on Terrorism"

The economy was already slowing when the tragic events of September 11, 2001 shook both the economy and nation's confidence. Still, the loss of 3,000 lives must be put in perspective—the world has lost as many lives on days like this before. Perhaps a slave ship sunk; perhaps a gas chamber worked overtime. Those who behave as if we have never seen loss of life like that on 9-11 ignore the principle of shared status that suggests that a life is a life, and that all life must be valued equally.

Similarly, the 9-11 relief funds exhibit our nation's class bias, and bias against working people. In other words, it has been reported that the family of a broker who once earned $150,000 will get millions of dollars in federal relief, while the family of a dishwasher who earned $20,000 will get just $400,000. While these are estimates that may vary with circumstances, the message is that government will value lives based on earnings. Insurance companies do that, and some workers were better insured than others! The federal government ought to embrace the principle of shared status and compensate families and survivors on some equal basis. Otherwise, their awards embrace the discrimination that people have experienced during their entire lives. It is said that people are all in the same boat, dying equally as the twin towers toppled. They may have died equally, but they didn't live equally, and debates around death benefits make this clear.

There are other race and class implications of the ways that the public has responded to September 11. Millions of dollars have been contributed to help victims, but thousands of charities that help people on the bottom are losing funds. Those who are hungry and homeless are somehow ignored as compassion shifts to 9-11 victims and their families. Further, public policy wants to bail out those industries affected by 9-11, but they don't want to bail out the people affected by industrial dislocation. Thus, airlines have a bailout fund of billions of dollars, but those who clean airports, or who work in hotels, or even who work for airlines, are not covered by bailout funds. Some are worthy of help, others are not. Workers who lost their jobs and livelihoods in the collapse of the Twin Towers will be helped, but peddlers who sold them fruit and coffee as they entered the building may have more difficulty documenting their need for help and receiving it.

Race, Class, and Enron

Class matters, which are clearly intertwined with race matters, will be the focus of discussion for the 107th Congress in the wake of the Enron bankruptcy. It was amazing to watch that company play the "wife card" in January, 2001, when Linda Lay told NBC reporter Lisa Myers that her family had "lost everything" and had little more than their ($7 million) home. Actually, the family owns more than a dozen properties, some of which are for sale. Kenneth Lay also holds more than $10 million in stock in companies other than Enron. There is a certain form of hubris that allows a family to take to the airwaves and plead poverty, even as their actions have impoverished thousands of Enron workers.

The Enron case is important to African Americans and other people of color because it is a textbook case on double standards. It suggests that the wealthy have differential access to politicians than others do, that they gain loans and credit through different lending standards, that they have different requirements for accounting, and even for declaring bankruptcy. It is ironic that as Enron has filed the nation's largest bankruptcy claim, credit card companies have been asking that Congress make it more difficult for the average American to declare bankruptcy. In legislation proposed in the spring of 2001, at a time when individual bankruptcies exceeded 1.2 million, and the average person filing for bankruptcy earned $22,000,[4] credit card companies asked that their repayments be prioritized—even over child support payments.

If African Americans had the access Enron had, we might have reparations by now. Enron is a plea for campaign finance reform, a reminder of the way the power pie is divided, and an illustration of the reasons that the gaps between African Americans and whites, between the haves and have nots, are so great. While senior Enron managers traded their stock, those who participated in the company's retirement plan, putting their own money into a company-administered 401(k) plan watched their savings evaporate as the stock price plummeted from a high of $70 a year ago to just 38 cents in January, 2002. For a 10-day period, when stock prices dropped by 20 percent, workers could not trade their stock because the pension administrator was being changed and transactions were frozen. Meanwhile, former CEO Kenneth Lay urged employees to buy stock in September 2001, even as he had sold tens of millions of dollars of stock of his own.

Yet according to the National Compensation Survey, which measured benefits available to workers in private companies, most people are not covered by retirement benefits. Just 48 percent of all Americans have either a defined benefit plan or a defined contribution plan, with the remainder relying on Social Security and their own savings for retirement. While 48 percent of all workers had employer contributions to a pension plan, just 32 percent of African Americans and 36 percent of Hispanics worked for companies that contributed to a pension plan. The Enron debacle reminds us of the differential economic status of African Americans and whites. The vast majority of African American workers, because of their occupational and industrial status, were not directly affected by this scandal. But those who had pensions with Enron suffered measurably.

How Long at the Periphery?

In recession and recovery, African Americans remain at the periphery of the economy. We are not full participants because of our differential incomes, differential wealth holding, and differential treatment in the labor market. The gaps persist even as the market fluctuates, and they are highlighted by exogenous shocks, like the events of September 11 and the bankruptcy of Enron. While there has been progress from a generation ago, African Americans are not "players" in the economy, especially when the interests of our community are being brokered.

This need not be a permanent situation. Tremendous resources exist in the African American community. According to Target Market News, which tracks African American spending and income, African American income stands at $543 billion as of 2001.[5] These funds can be more carefully directed, and used to support African American businesses. Increased African American economic leverage both closes gaps and moves people from the periphery into the mainstream of economic activity.

Equally importantly, it should be a focus of public policy to close the gaps that keep African Americans at the periphery. A policy focus on wealth-building improves the status of some African American people. These policies begin with efforts to improve educational access for African Americans, because those with the most education are able to garner greater earnings. Education is not enough, though. Policies that range from affirmative action to minority business set-asides empower those who are prepared to participate in the economic game. Were reparations realized, they would go a long way to close the wealth gap between African Americans and whites.

The structure of our nation's economy provides both opportunities and challenges for African Americans. The two clearest trends for the future are globalization and the proliferation of technology. African Americans lag in the technological game, with the digital divide narrower, but as real as it was a decade ago. According to Thomas P. Novak and Donna L. Hoffman of Vanderbilt University, authors of the 1998 article "Bridging the Digital Divide: The Impact of Race on Computer Access and Internet Use,"[6] 29 percent of African Americans have home computers, compared to 44 percent of whites. Moreover, while increasing numbers of African Americans are involved in the use of computers, computer access for African American youngsters lags behind that of white youngsters.

The trend toward globalization makes the African continent much more important than it was a decade ago in the context of world economic development. Yet too many Americans lack the global focus that would allow us to develop contacts with the rest of the world. African Americans are uniquely situated to develop our African ties and to expand aspects of our economic cooperation. In some ways, work on African development will improve the economic status of African Americans in the United States.

Still, the basic ways that African Americans can close gaps are tried and true. We must educate and participate, invest in our communities, increase our economic ownership. This must be a community priority, something that most African Americans focus on as passionately as we once focused on our voting rights. Our unequal status is only a given if we accept it. Both our activism and our commitment to gap-closing public policy move us from the periphery into the mainstream of our nation's economic life.

Make no mistake, that mainstream is a flawed one, and it is one that may well incorporate some of the inequalities that are inherent in a capitalist society. African Americans must be concerned with matters of class as much as we are concerned with matters of race. Will we be satisfied if median incomes between African Americans and whites are the same, even as millions of African Americans remain in poverty? Would we be as concerned about the minimum wage and home ownership gaps if median incomes were similar?

African American people have a mandate to fight for economic justice, a mandate that Dr. Martin Luther King, Jr. laid out in his Nobel Peace Prize acceptance speech when he said, "I have the audacity to believe that people everywhere will have three meals a day for their bodies, education and culture for their minds, peace and freedom for their spirits." Our mandate to fight is an important one as long as people live and survive at the economic periphery. As our economy evolves, it is important to view new challenges through the lens of race and class, to eradicate the notion of an economic periphery through both public policy intervention and through tried and true methods like economic boycotts.

1   All of the data in this section came from the United States Bureau of Census, *Current Population Survey, 2001* (Washington, D.C.).

2   Federal Reserve System of the United States, *Survey of Consumer Finance* (Washington, D.C., 1998).

3   Data for 2001 will be released in 2003.

4   SMR Research Corporation, *The Credit Risk Outlook for 2002* (Hackettstown, NJ: SMR Research Corporation, 2001).

5   Target Market News, *The Buying Power of Black America: 2001* (Chicago: Target Market News, 2001).

6   The working paper cited is a longer version of the article, "Bridging the Racial Divide on the Internet." It was originally published in *Science,* 17 April 1998.

Chapter 3

Blacks in the Labor Movement

Interview with Bill Fletcher Conducted by Herb Boyd

Herb Boyd: What is the key issue facing Blacks in the labor movement?

Bill Fletcher: In order to look at the condition of Black workers in the labor movement in the US one has to recognize that the labor movement since its inception in the 1830s has been divided over the issue of who should be included. The two earliest divisions were over the question of slavery and over the question of women. Believe it or not, there was one section that favored slavery, while the other opposed it. A third sector took a "hear no evil, see no evil" approach as a way of completely avoiding the issue. Within that framework, the issue of Black workers emerged as a critical sore spot. After the Civil War, the split reemerged over the question of whether or not the labor movement should be a white labor movement or represent a truly diverse and equitable mix of workers.

While in many cases the flashpoint was the question of Black workers, it wasn't just Black workers who were being discriminated against by a section of labor movement. Latinos, Chicanos, Native Americans, Chinese, as well as women, in many instances, were being excluded. What appears to be the psychology behind this exclusion was the notion that white male workers represented the relevant working class, and all others were peripheral. Thus, the objective of this section of organized labor was to increase the living standard of white male workers. But to borrow from Marx,

"Labor in white skin cannot be free so long as labor in black skin is enslaved." This was true, not just for Black workers, but for Chinese, Japanese, and Latino workers.

Now the response of Black workers is very interesting. After the Civil War there was a rash of organizing and strikes that took place in the South. Black workers began to fight for justice, dignity, and increased living standards. This paralleled a great upsurge led by Black women around the issue of education. On the national level, there were actions that led to the development of the Colored National Labor Union, under Isaac Myers. This was done in response to Black workers being excluded from the National Labor Union. The lengthy history from that period to now is that of one section of organized labor, which has been receptive to the inclusion of African Americans, other ethnic groups, women, and the unskilled versus the section that has been exclusive and restrictive. I think this dichotomy is very important because there are many people who have experiences with only the one sector of labor that is racist and exclusive, and they draw from this an impression that is not applicable to the entire labor movement.

Another point that's important to recognize is the response to this exclusion by workers of color and women—who often organized their own independent unions. This would be the character of things until the 1930s, which witnessed a number of pivotal moments. During this period, there was a coming together of different social forces that brought about a different kind of labor movement. When several unions split from the American Federation of Labor (AFL) and formed the Congress of Industrial Organizations (CIO), this effort was aimed at organizing the mass production workers in automobile, rubber, shipyards, etc. And in order for this effort to succeed, it needed the involvement of Black workers, Chicanos, and Asians, as well as whites. What is critical then, is that, in many cities of the country, workers of color played a pivotal role in deciding elections in favor of the CIO. The second thing is that in the African American community it was recognized that the CIO's approach—one of organizing all the workers irrespective of their race, color, gender, or ethnicity—was an opportunity to raise their living standards. So, hundreds of thousands Black workers entered the official labor movement. Now, while many people don't see it this way, unionization was probably the most effective antipoverty program this country has ever seen.

A third implication was the creation of a new echelon of Black leadership. Prior to the 1930s, leadership in the Black community tended to be dominated by forces from the middle strata—ministers, doctors, lawyers, teachers, and business people. What happened as a result of the 1930s and the 1940s was that there emerged a new wave of Black leaders, who, in many cases, played a role not only in the workplace, but also in the community. There are such examples as Velma Hopkins and Miranda Smith, who were labor leaders in Winston Salem, North Carolina with Local 22, Food, Tobacco, Agricultural and Allied Workers Union. Before her premature death, Smith was the southern director of the union and a member of the union's executive board, the highest position any Black woman had held in the labor movement up to that time. Another example is Coleman Young in Detroit. Young emerged as a leader with the United Automobile Workers and later with the National Negro Labor Council. By the early seventies, he was the mayor of the city. Out of the labor movement there emerged a number of significant leaders who became prominent in their communities. Unfortunately, many of these leaders have been ignored in our history texts.

In the sixties and the early seventies, there was another pivotal moment for the labor movement. At this time, there was a tumult of public sector organizing. Again, new leaders emerged. Moreover, there was a partnering of efforts between sections of labor and the civil rights and Black Power movements. For example, in Charleston, South Carolina in 1969, the efforts of Local 1199, the National Health and Hospital Workers, to organize workers were in alliance with the Southern Christian Leadership Conference (SCLC). Other similar initiatives occurred in Florida and of course in Memphis, where Dr. King was murdered. One of the things I should add here is that the seventies and the early eighties were devastating periods for Black workers in a number of ways. When the seventies' economic recession hit, it had a disproportionate impact on the Black workforce. With the advent of so-called deindustrialization, which might be better termed the "deurbanization of industry," many of the highly paid, unionized employers, where African American workers were often found, moved to other areas, particularly to rural locations that were largely white. These areas were barely accessible to workers of color. One of the effects of this was to weaken the role of Black unionized workers in various communities, but also within the labor movement as a whole.

We should also note the large upsurge of caucuses—not just Black workers. Of course, we can't ignore the impact of the League of Revolutionary Black Workers at this time. To some extent, these actions represented the fusion of Black Power movement and militancy with worker insurgency. Wildcat strikes, sentiments against the Vietnam War, and other protests against social injustice were having an impact on organized labor. When the recession hit, unemployment began to grow. This had a chilling effect on the insurgency, and this was compounded by layoffs. Having said all this, there are some things we must keep in mind. One is that African Americans, contrary to common knowledge, have a greater percentage of our people in unions than any other ethnic group. I don't mean by this that Blacks comprise a majority, but merely to say that 18 percent of Blacks are union members. We represent almost 15 percent of organized labor, which is nothing to sneeze at. This means we comprise a significant bloc within organized labor, which if organized, could have an important impact on the labor movement as a whole.

Boyd: Given this significant representation in the labor movement, what percentage do Blacks have at the leadership level?

Fletcher: I tried to find some statistics on this but I was unable. But I can say, anecdotally, that we are underrepresented in the leadership of organized labor. When the new leadership took over the AFL-CIO in October, 1995, the executive council increased the number of women and people of color. You have on the council now people like Bill Lucy, secretary-treasurer of the American Federation of State, County and Municipal Employees (AFSCME); Clayola Brown, vice president of the Union of Needles Trade Industrial Technical Employees (UNITE!); Gloria

Johnson, vice president of the International Brotherhood of Electrical Workers (IBEW), that recently merged with the Communications Workers of America (CWA); Joe Green, who is the president of American Federation of School Administrators (AFSA); Leon Lynch, vice president of United Steel Workers of America (USWA); Carol Haynes, who is the president of a Teamsters local in New York and on the executive council; Gene Upshaw, of the Federation of Professional Athletes (FPA), and there are other people of color on the executive council. This has been a very important development in the last several years. As for leadership of the unions themselves, well, we've still got a long way to go in terms of greater representation. But the problem here is dealing with the dynamics that occur within each union. To remedy this situation, Black workers in each of these different unions have to elevate and engage in coalition politics in order to get elected to leadership positions.

This does not mean, however, that Black workers and other workers of color should tone down their fight on racism in order to get elected. No. We need to be able to identify allies who can help us get elected. And those allies must understand that the candidates are rainbow candidates, and I mean rainbow with a small "r." And that these candidates will fight for racial justice and other issues, such as where should the union be going over the next several decades. These are issues that Black workers need to be speaking to, not just issues particular to them. This is one of the big challenges we continue to face. One alliance we really need to develop is with Latino workers, and with Asian workers. We need to be paying attention to these groups that are growing as a percentage of the workforce. One of the things I'm very heartbroken about is that in places in the country like California, all too many Black labor leaders pay precious little attention to uniting with Latinos. They basically have a view of ethnic politics as opposed to rainbow politics. Essentially, they seem to be saying, "Let's cut the best deal we can, while we can still do it." They don't appear to understand that they can strengthen themselves by uniting.

Boyd: Has there been any interest expressed by Latino leaders to unite with Black workers?

Fletcher: Yes, but we also have to recognize that there are tendencies toward ethnic politics in those groups too. I have Chicano colleagues, for example, who have told me straight out that one of the things they hear among some backward Chicano leaders is "Why do we need Black workers now? Our numbers are growing, why do we need them? They haven't done anything for us." This is very scary because what I begin to see is something akin to the former Yugoslavia, rather than some kind of fusion.

Boyd: There appears to be a large Black membership in local and municipal unions, such as AFSCME, Local 1199, DC37; to what extent do they participate in the leadership of these unions?

Fletcher: There is a very significant presence of Blacks in the leadership of these unions, where Black workers have been playing a very important role for years. But the one thing we must say, and it's a sad story looking at District Council 37 in New York City, it's not a matter of color but integrity and what their politics are. There has been an unfortunate situation of corruption there, or at least allegations of corruption among leaders who espouse very progressive rhetoric. All of this has been very tragic and demoralizing. You are talking about leaders who, for the most part, were very well respected but who allegedly had their hands in the cookie jar. They should have assumed that by being Black they were under more scrutiny than whites. Any Black person who doesn't keep this in mind is living in a fool's paradise. Furthermore, when we get leadership positions we should understand that we are not there for our own self-enrichment but to represent the members. We can never lose sight of that.

Boyd: How did so-called welfare reform, initiated by former President Clinton, impact the working class?

Fletcher: As I like to say, there was no welfare reform. It was welfare repeal. First of all, over the last couple of years people have been saying that "welfare reform is so good, people are doing so well." But let's take a closer look at the situation. The economy has been rocking and rolling along to the benefit, we should add, of the wealthy, upper-class 10 or 20 percent, not so much the bottom 80 percent. There has been no recession and there have been jobs, but mainly low-paying ones that can be filled by welfare recipients. The real test—and there have been some studies on this—will be when these various programs and their time limits expire. When welfare was replaced by workfare, the idea was that you could be on these programs three or four years and that was it. That was it for a lifetime. When these programs expire, what's going to happen? We don't know. What's going to happen when there's a recession? We don't know. But we do know that under capitalism there will be a recession. We've had a long period of expansion for a whole host of reasons, and this expansion has been domestic. Keep in mind there was a crash in Asia that affected the lives of millions of people. Half of this world right now is enduring a recession, or in some cases a depression. There are one billion people on the planet unemployed or underemployed. When the recession comes, we can guess that many of the people that are welfare recipients will be pushed into a pauper-like status. At that juncture, it's anyone's guess what will happen. It will be incumbent on the union at that moment to figure out ways of organizing people in this extreme level of poverty. We will probably have organizations of the unemployed the likes of which we haven't seen since the thirties. There will be a need to link with welfare rights organizations, like the Kensington Welfare Rights Union. The clock is ticking.

Boyd: Can we expect class hostility between the increasing large Black middle class and the so-called underclass?

Fletcher: The short answer is yes. Not only can we expect it, we can see it happening already. Let me give you an example. Black Entertainment Television (BET) and its founder and CEO Bob Johnson, who is the darling of liberal circles and who is viewed by many people in Black America as a paragon of virtue, has a few warts. I am concerned about his open hostility to unionization, which was evidenced in a few ways just recently. One incident occurred right here in Washington, D.C., with his hostility to the unionization of the International Brotherhood of Electrical Workers (IBEW). Another obvious example of this hostility was put forth by Black comedians about a year or so ago. They were being paid a flat rate of $150 to participate in one of his shows, and this did not cover the comedians' expenses, such as travel and accommodations. This sparked a massive outcry from segments of the Black community. A number of notables such as Jay Leno, Tom Joyner, and Richard Pryor expressed their concern about this. This was a clear case that class struggle was erupting in the Black community. Even the official publications owned by Black Americans seldom provide coverage of Black working class leaders. *Black Enterprise*, for example, realizing it's an organ of Black capital, gives a pretense of speaking for Black America and its up and coming leaders. Obviously they are going to pay attention to Black entrepreneurs and business leaders, that's their main objective, but they go beyond this and talk about lawyers, Black leaders in the entertainment industry, medicine and media, sports and what have you. But when it comes to the Black working class, there is very little discussion. This neglect has a long history, all the way back to the twenties and thirties when A. Philip Randolph was organizing the sleeping car porters, and the Black media had a very ambivalent attitude toward him as a Black working class leader. I would expect we're going to see more of this class hostility among African Americans. When I visit college campuses and speak with Black students, particularly at Black colleges and universities, you see very little consciousness of unionization.

Boyd: Are these students picking up the message from the media about the ineffectiveness of unions, that the numbers are decreasing and why bother?

Fletcher: No, I think they are picking up a different kind of message. I don't think they understand what unions are. They seem to feel that unions were important during an earlier period, but not anymore; that we have risen to a point now where you can make it if you try, and that the best route is one of entrepreneurship. I think they are also picking up that this notion of collective struggle and action is a thing of the past. That might have been good in the previous decades, but now, they seem to feel, it's about making money, and that the only way you can have an impact on future Black America is by setting up a business.

Boyd: Would this outlook be, to some extent, affected by what part of the country these young people come from, and whether there was a history of struggle in their community such as those who rallied in Seattle against the World Trade Organization...?

Fletcher: Certainly that has an impact. The struggle against globalization definitely had an impact on the consciousness of the people in this country across the board, but the problem with the struggle around globalization is that people of color have not been particularly visible or active. In other words, I don't think Black activists, with certain notable exceptions, have paid enough attention to the process of rebuilding a liberation tendency or class politics within our movement.

Boyd: Regarding again the burgeoning gulf between the Black middle class and the so-called underclass, is the manifestation of crime another aspect of the increasingly prevalent class hostility?

Fletcher: Yes, because I think what's happening is that rather than seeing the Black working class as part of Black America, there is an emerging Black class stratum that have decided that these are "other" people—the old "us and them" dichotomy. I would not, however, go as far as people such as William Julius Wilson, who has argued that the problem is the Black middle class moving out of the community which has led to the weakening of the living standards in our community. What I believe has happened is that sections of the Black working class have collapsed. That the jobs of many Black working class people that produced a living standard which allowed them to buy a home and put their children through college have moved, businesses have closed down. So, it's not that the Black middle class has moved out, though there certainly has been some indication of "Black flight," but that there's been a devastating impact on Black America due to the restructuring of the economy.

Sure, it's true, some segments of the Black middle class have moved out to gated and guarded communities, and all you have to do is look at a community like Prince George's County in Maryland. Here you have the highest per capita income in Black America. It also has this incredible rash of police brutality, but a low level of mobilization against it. Why? I think part of what has happened is that many segments of the Black middle class community in Prince George's County are so glad to be there that they don't want to rock the boat. They are putting their heads in the sand, hoping and praying they can get over it. This is leading to a very bad situation.

Boyd: "Black workers take the lead" used to be a popular slogan. Does it have any validity today? Where are the veterans of the labor struggles of the recent past who played such a visible role in the League of Revolutionary Black Workers, Black Workers Congress, Dodge Revolutionary Union Movement (DRUM), and others?

Fletcher: "Black workers take the lead" was a slogan that emerged in the late sixties and early seventies that has a number of different interpretations. One interpretation was that Black workers should be given the leadership of the African American movement. Another interpretation was that Black workers needed to lead the working class. So it depends on how one interprets this slogan. But if you put it all in its best light, I would say there is a dire need for Black workers to lead the African American movement and to play a leadership role in the labor movement. But what is generally happening is that the Black middle stratum has been the group that has led and set the terms for Black America. This is essentially the Black entrepreneurial segment and consequently it will only have a small number of Black folks. Most Black workers do not work for Black-owned companies. Most Black workers will be employed by governmental agencies or white-owned businesses. Black workers, as I see it, should shape the future of Black America, and in that sense "Black workers take the lead" is a valuable slogan.

Boyd: To what degree has the Black Radical Congress (BRC) inherited the militancy of the Black working class, if it has?

Fletcher: I would say the BRC has the potential to inherit it. That it has within its ranks, and as part of its soul, the interest of the Black working class and a desire to base the BRC within the Black working class.

Chapter 4

Don't Dump on Us

The Environmental Justice Movement

Charles E. Simmons

One of the major differences between the traditional environmental/conservation movement, which gained steam in the US in the 1960s and '70s, and the environmental justice movement, which dates back to the early '80s, is that traditional environmentalism has generally focused on the impact of pollution on wildlife, air, and water.

The environmental justice movement focuses on the hazardous impact of pollutants on the human habitat, especially the urban communities where people of color and poor and working-class folks live. And in many communities, the people who are responsible for children—parents, grandparents, and extended family members—are the activists who are leading environmental justice (EJ) campaigns. Motivated by concerns about the health of their children and grandchildren, these activists have deep roots in the community and churches, and are able to mobilize support and interest in their cause, often through personal connections.

Yet, this grassroots movement also boasts civil rights activists and scholars with international reputations who are advocates for the local communities they study and write about.

What issues have created these coalitions? In *Confronting Environmental Racism*, the pathbreaking anthology edited by Robert Bullard, Minister Benjamin Chavis Muhammad observes:

People of color bear the brunt of the nation's pollution problem

. . . . Environmental racism is racial discrimination in environmental policy making. It is racial discrimination in the enforcement of regulations and laws. It is racial discrimination in the deliberate targeting of communities of color for toxic waste disposal and the citing or polluting industries. It is racial discrimination in the official sanctioning of the life-threatening presence of poisons and pollutants in communities of color. And it is racial discrimination in the history of excluding people of color from the mainstream environmental groups, decision-making boards, commissions and regulatory bodies.[1]

A Turning Point

The First National People of Color Environmental Leadership Summit, sponsored by the United Church of Christ and held October 1991 in Washington D.C., brought together some 1000 grassroots activists from most of the 50 states—including Hawaii—and also Puerto Rico, Mexico, and the Marshall Islands. This conference was a major step in the development of the Environmental Justice Movement.[2]

The delegates prepared 17 principles which codified the movement's spirit and goals. The principles, formally adopted by the summit, are:

1. Environmental justice affirms the sacredness of Mother Earth, ecological unity, and the interdependence of all species, and the right to be free from ecological destruction.

2. Environmental justice demands that public policy be based on mutual respect and justice for all peoples, free from any form of discrimination or bias.

3. Environmental justice mandates the right to ethical, balanced and responsible uses of land and renewable resources in the interest of a sustainable planet for humans and other living things.

4. Environmental justice calls for universal protection from nuclear testing, extraction, production, and disposal of toxic/hazardous wastes and poisons and nuclear testing that threaten the fundamental right to clean air, land, water, and food.

5. Environmental justice affirms the fundamental right to political, economic, cultural, and environmental self-determination

of all peoples.

6. Environmental justice demands the cessation of the production of all toxins, hazardous wastes, and radioactive materials, and that all past and current producers be held strictly accountable to the people for detoxification and the containment at the point of production.

7. Environmental justice demands the right to participate as equal partners at every level of decision-making including needs assessment, planning, implementation, enforcement and evaluation.

8. Environmental justice affirms the right of all workers to a safe and healthy work environment, without being forced to choose between an unsafe livelihood and unemployment. It also affirms the right of those who work at home to be free from environmental hazards.

9. Environmental justice protects the right of victims of environmental injustice to receive full compensation and reparations for damages as well as quality health care.

10. Environmental justice considers governmental acts of environmental injustice a violation of international law, the Universal Declaration On Human Rights, and the United Nations Convention on Genocide.

11. Environmental justice must recognize a special legal and natural relationship of Native Peoples to the US government through treaties, agreements, compacts, and covenants affirming sovereignty and self-determination.

12. Environmental justice affirms the need for urban and rural ecological policies to clean up and rebuild our cities and rural areas in balance with nature, honoring the cultural integrity of all our communities, and providing fair access for all to the full range of resources.

13. Environmental justice calls for the strict enforcement of principles of informed consent and a halt to the testing of experimental reproductive and medical procedures and vaccinations on people of color.

14. Environmental justice opposes the destructive operations of multi-national corporations.

15. Environmental justice opposes military occupation, repression, and exploitation of lands, peoples, and cultures, and other life forms.

16. Environmental justice calls for the education of present and future generations which emphasizes social and environmental issues, based on our experience and an appreciation of our diverse cultural perspectives.

17. Environmental justice requires that we, as individuals, make personal and consumer choices to consume as little of Mother Earth's resources and to produce as little waste as possible; and make the conscious decision to challenge and reprioritize our lifestyles to insure the health of the natural world for present and future generations.[3]

Charles Lee, a pioneer in the UCC Environmental Justice Commission for Racial Justice, said of the Summit, "it expanded into an international struggle for public health, cultural survival and sovereignty of Native and indigenous peoples, land rights, land use, community empowerment, transportation, energy, federal facilities cleanup, and defense conversion, urban decay, economic justice, sustainability, and trans-boundary issues."[4]

E proponents identified environmental justice not only as a civil right, but as a human right, and began to establish networks with similar activists around the planet.

Environmental Justice and Public Health

One of the most crucial challenges faced by E activists in the US is the prevalence of asthma among children and senior citizens who live in the inner cities. Not surprisingly, numerous studies have revealed the link between high asthma rates and high rates of air pollution. According to Robert Bullard, Director of the Environmental Justice Resource Center at Clark Atlanta University, "Asthma accounts for 10 million missed school days, 1.2 million emergency room visits, 15 million outpatient visits, and half a million hospitalizations each year."[5]

In the inner city, children have the highest rates for asthma prevalence, hospitalization, and mortality. A report from the Children's Defense Fund (CDF) indicates that asthma is growing among inner city youth at an alarming rate.[6] It is the most common chronic disease of childhood and the fourth leading cause of disability among children less than 18 years of age in the US.[7] In every age group, Blacks have higher rates for asthma-related emergency room visits and hospitalizations than do whites. As of 1998, according to the CDF, "African Americans are almost three times more likely than whites to die from asthma."[8]

Although health care providers say that asthma can be reduced by decreasing exposures to allergens and pollutants, it can be extremely difficult for parents with limited incomes to make these efforts on behalf of their children. In 1995, at least 18 million children lived in areas where the air quality was below federal standards.[9] The major sources of air pollution include coal-burning power plants, oil and chemical refineries, incinerators, cars, buses and manufacturing sites. Inside the home and school, children confront another group of hazardous substances, including household or industrial cleaners, paint fumes, glue, asbestos, lead-based paint, or dust. According to the Children's Defense Fund, children are more susceptible to toxins and other environmental hazards.[10]

In addition, 3 to 4 million children live within a mile of one of the nation's most serious hazardous waste disposal sites, which are too often located near or in communities of color.[11] Those sites do not include the many commercial or illegal dump-sites that exist throughout these communities. The health effects of many of the chemicals have not been studied, but some of these substances cause respiratory problems, harm to the brain and nervous system and abnormal development. According to the Children's Defense Fund, "It may affect their intelligence, language ability, and attention span; make them restless and moody; and lead to behavioral and social problems."[12]

Detroit: A Case Study

More than 125 years of intense industrialization has been a curse and a blessing for the Motor City. In the 1940s, '50s, and '60s,

Detroit offered unskilled industrial laborers high wages, and spawned several important civil rights and labor organizations. But the economic downturns of the '70s and '80s were hard on the city's working class residents. Large areas of land once occupied by the auto industry giants and their suppliers are now giant dumps called "brown fields" and have created a heavy toxic burden for the community.

Detroiters and residents of the surrounding area throughout southeastern Michigan and neighboring Ontario, Canada, face other environmental challenges. During the tenure of popular mayor Coleman Young, the world's largest municipal incinerator was built. The Henry Ford Hospital, one of the state's largest medical institutions, is located within the same five-mile radius, in a residential area populated largely by African Americans. Until June 2001, the hospital burned medical waste, including body parts, on its premises. Local scholars have documented a high incidence of asthma, cancer, and respiratory ailments in the area closest to incinerators.[13] Lead, cadmium, and mercury are also prevalent, and there is an abundance of asbestos in the area's old buildings.

Bunyan Bryant, a professor at the University of Michigan and Elaine Hockman, a professor at Wayne State University, have studied the location of hazardous waste in the state, and they show a relationship between hazardous waste and incidents of low birth weight babies.[14]

It gets worse. State authorities release regular fish advisories about the Great Lakes waterway, warning residents about the danger of eating the fish throughout the region as a result of long-term pollution. According to one such fish advisory issued in 1999 by the Michigan Department of Community Health, (MDCH):

> The amounts of chemicals found in Michigan fish are not known to cause immediate sickness. But chemicals can collect in the body over time. It may take months or years of regularly eating contaminated fish to build up amounts that are a health concern. Chemicals may eventually affect your health or that of your children. Mothers who eat highly contaminated fish before birth may have children who are slower to develop and learn. A pregnant woman may pass these chemicals to her unborn child and

to the new baby through breast milk.[15]

Yet, some in our community are fighting against the environmental movement. An op-ed piece in the rabidly anti-EJ and anti-social justice *Michigan Chronicle* signed by three clergy members asked: "Is Environmental Justice Tyranny?" They suggested that African Americans are being ill-served by the environmental justice movement. From their perspective, jobs and contracts must come before health, particularly when they don't believe there is a health threat. Have they read the myriad of studies by public health departments around the country, or seen the data from the Children's Defense Fund? (Our short answer to Job Blackmail is this: "You can't work if you can't breathe!")

Where Do We Go From Here?

A major community and environmental victory was achieved in the summer of 2001, when, as a result of community pressure and protest, the Henry Ford Hospital shut down its incinerator.[16] The Henry Ford Hospital had been granted a consent order by the county authorities that allowed the hospital to continue using the incinerator if it reduced the pollution to levels acceptable to the Environmental Protection Administration (EPA). But that agreement was successfully challenged by environmental and community groups on the grounds that the EPA standards are lower than those of hospitals nationwide, and that better technology to recycle waste, like steam sterilization, exists today.

Another bright spot is emerging in one long-neglected community in Detroit called Northwest Goldberg. Neighborhood parents, grandparents, youth, and community activists in the "Committee for the Political Resurrection of Detroit" are embarking on a plan for from-the-bottom, sustainable community development. College students are working with high school and middle school students to publish a community newspaper that will focus on constructive projects completed by young people. Elementary students are working with college students to prepare murals for their building. The theme of the art work is "What Do I Want My Neighborhood and City to Look Like?" A youth choir will bring the young folks together for the first time in the spirit of empowerment.

Rank-and-file auto workers are being recruited to help with renovation of old homes. Students are conducting research to find alternative means of low-income housing development and local manufacturing that will employ neighbors and avoid the long-distance transportation needs. An internal transportation system is being studied for the use of seniors and workers. The local library basement is the site of a plant nursery for the community. Neighbors intend to give a used bicycle for every youth in the community and have a repair shop where they can be taught to fix the bikes. In planning is a system of community money to barter legally for goods and services for those outside of the economic system who have skills but no jobs and those who have needs but no money. And neighbors and activists of all ages are working shoulder to shoulder on weekends to clean up illegal dump sites and transform them into community gardens and recreation spaces, utilizing discarded materials such as painted old tires for beautification.

Nationally, a coalition of 29 EJ organizations in 2001 called for the Bush administration to take immediate and just steps on climate change policy that takes into consideration the needs of people of color, the poor, and working people. Designated the Environmental Justice and Climate Change Initiative (EJCC), this coalition supports energy efficiency, renewable energy, and conservation policies while seeking equitable measures to protect and assist the communities most affected by climate change.

In the future, we must continue to educate ourselves about developing sustainable cities, and also find ways to incorporate this education into all curricula, from kindergarten to university courses. Encourage our community activists to declare moratoriums on the big development schemes while we move to develop small and environmentally friendly community projects. Among this new education, we must abandon the idea that anything can be "thrown away" because there is no AWAY. Everything we discard returns to us in one form or another and may cause future problems if we do not recycle it in the first place.

In all of our struggles for sustainable communities, we must keep in mind that we have a human right to clean air, water and land, and continue to reflect upon the 17 Principles of Environmental Justice and bring these ideals to every school, church and neighborhood block club.

When we need to communicate our ideas or learn about new developments, let us keep in mind that it is the community or alternative media, which has a history of support and leadership for the struggle for justice.

We need new ideas about how to develop our communities and cities, and the old top-down method of leadership has not worked for us. Let us encourage our youth to join in this struggle. They can work, learn, and grow while contributing to the well-being of their communities.

As the 60,000 social justice activists and participants from around this embattled planet proclaimed in Porto Alegre, Brazil in 2002, "Another World Is Possible."

1   Benjamin F. Chavis, "Preface," in Robert Bullard (ed.), *Confronting Environmental Racism: Voices from the Grassroots* (Boston: South End Press, 1993), 3.

2   Ibid, 4.

3   For more information, see http://www.igc.org/saepj/Principles.html or http://www.ejnet.org/ej/ platform.html.

4   United Church of Christ Commission for Racial Justice, *The First National People of Color Environmental Leadership Summit: Program Guide* (New York: United Church of Christ, 1992).

5   Children's Defense Fund, *Yearbook 2000: The State of America's Children,* (Washington, DC: Children's Defense Fund) 37-41.

6   Ibid.

7   D. Almasi, "Earth Day, No Holiday for Black Americans: Anti-Minority Environmental Policies," *The Michigan Chronicle,* April 28-May 4, 1999, A-7.

8   Children's Defense Fund, *Yearbook 2000: The State of America's Children,* (Washington, DC: Children's Defense Fund) 37-41.

9   Ibid.

10 Ibid.

11 Ibid.

12 Ibid.

13 Ron Siegal, "Henry Ford Incinerator: A Case of Environmental Racism?" *The Michigan Citizen,* March 14-20, 1999, A-1, 8.

14 Bunyan Bryant and Elaine Hockman, "Hazardous Waste and Spatial Relations According to Race and Income in the State of Michigan," unpublished paper, 1994.

15 Michigan Department of Community Health, *Michigan Fish Advisory: Important Facts to Know if You Eat Michigan Fish* (Lansing: Government Press, 1999).

16 The Henry Ford Hospital System operates other hospitals in suburban Detroit. However, none of these hospitals burn waste in area incinerators. Instead, they send the waste out to processors who use environmentally friendly disposal processes.

Chapter 5

Masked Racism

Reflections on the Prison Industrial Complex

Angela Y. Davis

This article originally appeared in the Fall 1998 issue of *ColorLines*
Magazine.

Imprisonment has become the response of first resort to far
too many of the social problems that burden people who are
ensconced in poverty. These problems often are veiled by being
conveniently grouped together under the category "crime" and
by the automatic attribution of criminal behavior to people of
color. Homelessness, unemployment, drug addiction, mental ill-
ness, and illiteracy are only a few of the problems that disappear
from public view when the human beings contending with them
are relegated to cages.

Prisons thus perform a feat of magic. Or rather, the people
who continually vote in new prison bonds and tacitly assent to a
proliferating network of prisons and jails have been tricked into believing in the magic of imprisonment. But prisons do not disappear
problems, they disappear human beings. And the practice of disap-
pearing vast numbers of people from poor, immigrant, and racially
marginalized communities literally has become big business.

The seeming effortlessness of magic always conceals an enormous amount of behind-the-scenes work. When prisons disappear
human beings in order to convey the illusion of solving social
problems, penal infrastructures must be created to accommodate a
rapidly swelling population of caged people. Goods and services

must be provided to keep imprisoned populations alive. Sometimes these populations must be kept busy and at other times—particularly in repressive supermaximum prisons and in Immigration and Naturalization Service (INS) detention centers—they must be deprived of virtually all meaningful activity. Vast numbers of handcuffed and shackled people are moved across state borders as they are transferred from one state or federal prison to another.

All this work, which used to be the primary province of government, is now also performed by private corporations, whose links to government in the field of what is euphemistically called "corrections" resonate dangerously with the military industrial complex. The dividends that accrue from investment in the punishment industry, like those that accrue from investment in weapons production, only amount to social destruction. Taking into account the structural similarities and profitability of business-government linkages in the realms of military production and public punishment, the expanding penal system can now be characterized as a "prison industrial complex."

The Color of Imprisonment

Almost two million people are currently locked up in the immense network of US prisons and jails. More than 70 percent of the imprisoned population are people of color. It is rarely acknowledged that the fastest growing group of prisoners are Black women and that Native American prisoners are the largest group per capita. Approximately five million people—including those on probation and parole—are directly under the surveillance of the criminal justice system.

Three decades ago, the imprisoned population was approximately one-eighth its current size. While women still constitute a relatively small percentage of people behind bars, today the number of incarcerated women in California alone is almost twice what the nationwide women's prison population was in 1970. According to Elliott Currie, "The prison has become a looming presence in our society to an extent unparalleled in our history—or that of any other industrial democracy. Short of major wars, mass incarceration has been the most thoroughly implemented government social program of our time."

To deliver up bodies destined for profitable punishment, the political economy of prisons relies on racialized assumptions of criminality—such as images of Black welfare mothers reproducing criminal children—and on racist practices in arrest, conviction, and sentencing patterns. Colored bodies constitute the main human raw material in this vast experiment to disappear the major social problems of our time. Once the aura of magic is stripped away from the imprisonment solution, what is revealed is racism, class bias, and the parasitic seduction of capitalist profit. The prison industrial system materially and morally impoverishes its inhabitants and devours the social wealth needed to address the very problems that have led to spiraling numbers of prisoners.

As prisons take up more and more space on the social landscape, other government programs that have previously sought to respond to social needs—such as Temporary Assistance to Needy Families—are being squeezed out of existence. The deterioration of public education, including prioritizing discipline and security over learning in public schools located in poor communities, is directly related to the prison "solution."

Profiting from Prisoners

As prisons proliferate in US society, private capital has become enmeshed in the punishment industry. And, precisely because of their profit potential, prisons are becoming increasingly important to the US economy. If the notion of punishment as a source of potentially stupendous profits is disturbing by itself, then the strategic dependence on racist structures and ideologies to render mass punishment palatable and profitable is even more troubling.

Prison privatization is the most obvious instance of capital's current movement toward the prison industry. While government-run prisons are often in gross violation of international human rights standards, private prisons are even less accountable. In March of this year, the Corrections Corporation of America (CCA), the largest US private prison company, claimed 54,944 beds in 68 facilities under contract or development in the US,

Puerto Rico, the United Kingdom, and Australia. Following the global trend of subjecting more women to public punishment, CCA recently opened a women's prison outside Melbourne. The company recently identified California as its "new frontier."

Wackenhut Corrections Corporation (WCC), the second largest US prison company, claimed contracts and awards to manage 46 facilities in North America, the UK, and Australia. It boasts a total of 30,424 beds as well as contracts for prisoner health care services, transportation, and security.

Currently, the stocks of both CCA and WCC are doing extremely well. Between 1996 and 1997, CCA's revenues increased by 58 percent, from $293 million to $462 million. Its net profit grew from $30.9 million to $53.9 million. WCC raised its revenues from $138 million in 1996 to $210 million in 1997. Unlike public correctional facilities, the vast profits of these private facilities rely on the employment of non-union labor.

The Prison Industrial Complex

But private prison companies are only the most visible component of the increasing corporatization of punishment. Government contracts to build prisons have bolstered the construction industry. The architectural community has identified prison design as a major new niche. Technology developed for the military by companies like Westinghouse is being marketed for use in law enforcement and punishment.

Moreover, corporations that appear to be far removed from the business of punishment are intimately involved in the expansion of the prison industrial complex. Prison construction bonds are one of the many sources of profitable investment for leading financiers such as Merrill Lynch. MCI charges prisoners and their families outrageous prices for the precious telephone calls which are often the only contact prisoners have with the free world.

Many corporations whose products we consume on a daily basis have learned that prison labor power can be as profitable as third world labor power exploited by US-based global corporations. Both relegate formerly unionized workers to joblessness and many even wind up in prison. Some of the companies that use prison labor are IBM, Motorola, Compaq, Texas Instruments, Honcywell, Microsoft, and Boeing. But it is not only the high-tech industries that reap the profits of prison labor. Nordstrom department stores sell jeans that are marketed as "Prison Blues," as well as T-shirts and jackets made in Oregon prisons. The advertising slogan for these clothes is "made on the inside to be worn on the outside." Maryland prisoners inspect glass bottles and jars used by Revlon and Pierre Cardin, and schools throughout the world buy graduation caps and gowns made by South Carolina prisoners.

"For private business," write Eve Goldberg and Linda Evans (a political prisoner inside the Federal Correctional Institution at Dublin, California) "prison labor is like a pot of gold. No strikes. No union organizing. No health benefits, unemployment insurance, or workers' compensation to pay. No language barriers, as in foreign countries. New leviathan prisons are being built with thousands of eerie acres of factories inside the walls. Prisoners do data entry for Chevron, make telephone reservations for TWA, raise hogs, shovel manure, make circuit boards, limousines, waterbeds, and lingerie for Victoria's Secret—all at a fraction of the cost of 'free labor.' "

Devouring the Social Wealth

Although prison labor—which ultimately is compensated at a rate far below the minimum wage—is hugely profitable for the private companies that use it, the penal system as a whole does not produce wealth. It devours the social wealth that could be used to subsidize housing for the homeless, to ameliorate public education for poor and racially marginalized communities, to open free drug rehabilitation programs for people who wish to kick their habits, to create a national health care system, to expand programs to combat HIV, to eradicate domestic abuse—and, in the process, to create well-paying jobs for the unemployed.

Since 1984 more than twenty new prisons have opened in California, while only one new campus was added to the California State University system and none to the University of California system. In 1996–97, higher education received only 8.7 percent of the state's General Fund while corrections received 9.6 percent.

Now that affirmative action has been declared illegal in California, it is obvious that education is increasingly reserved for certain people, while prisons are reserved for others. Five times as many Black men are presently in prison as in four-year colleges and universities. This new segregation has dangerous implications for the entire country.

By segregating people labeled as criminals, prison simultaneously fortifies and conceals the structural racism of the US economy. Claims of low unemployment rates—even in Black communities—make sense only if one assumes that the vast numbers of people in prison have really disappeared and thus have no legitimate claims to jobs. The numbers of Black and Latino men currently incarcerated amount to two percent of the male labor force. According to criminologist David Downes, "Treating incarceration as a type of hidden unemployment may raise the jobless rate for men by about one-third, to 8 percent. The effect on the black labor force is greater still, raising the [Black] male unemployment rate from 11 percent to 19 percent."

Hidden Agenda

Mass incarceration is not a solution to unemployment, nor is it a solution to the vast array of social problems that are hidden away in a rapidly growing network of prisons and jails. However, the great majority of people have been tricked into believing in the efficacy of imprisonment, even though the historical record clearly demonstrates that prisons do not work. Racism has undermined our ability to create a popular critical discourse to contest the ideological trickery that posits imprisonment as key to public safety. The focus of state policy is rapidly shifting from social welfare to social control.

Black, Latino, Native American, and many Asian youth are portrayed as purveyors of violence, traffickers of drugs, and as envious of commodities that they have no right to possess. Young Black and Latina women are represented as sexually promiscuous and as indiscriminately propagating babies and poverty. Criminality and deviance are racialized. Surveillance is thus focused on communities of color, immigrants, the unemployed, the undereducated, the homeless, and in general on those who have a diminishing claim to social resources. Their claim to social resources continues to diminish in large part because law enforcement and penal measures increasingly devour these resources. The prison industrial complex has thus created a vicious cycle of punishment which only further impoverishes those whose impoverishment is supposedly "solved" by imprisonment.

Therefore, as the emphasis of government policy shifts from social welfare to crime control, racism sinks more deeply into the economic and ideological structures of US society. Meanwhile, conservative crusaders against affirmative action and bilingual education proclaim the end of racism, while their opponents suggest that racism's remnants can be dispelled through dialogue and conversation. But conversations about "race relations" will hardly dismantle a prison industrial complex that thrives on and nourishes the racism hidden within the deep structures of our society.

The emergence of a US prison industrial complex within a context of cascading conservatism marks a new historical moment, whose dangers are unprecedented. But so are its opportunities. Considering the impressive number of grassroots projects that continue to resist the expansion of the punishment industry, it ought to be possible to bring these efforts together to create radical and nationally visible movements that can legitimize anticapitalist critiques of the prison industrial complex. It ought to be possible to build movements in defense of prisoners' human rights and movements that persuasively argue that what we need is not new prisons, but new health care, housing, education, drug programs, jobs, and education. To safeguard a democratic future, it is possible and necessary to weave together the many and increasing strands of resistance to the prison industrial complex into a powerful movement for social transformation.

Chapter 6

Race and Gender

bell hooks

This excerpt is from *Feminism Is for Everybody: Passionate Politics* (Cambridge: South End Press, 2000).

No intervention changed the face of American feminism more than the demand that feminist thinkers acknowledge the reality of race and racism. All white women in this nation know that their status is different from that of black women/women of color. They know this from the time they are little girls watching television and seeing only their images, and looking at magazines and seeing only their images. They know that the only reason nonwhites are absent/invisible is because they are not white. All white women in this nation know that whiteness is a privileged category. The fact that white females may choose to repress or deny this knowledge does not mean they are ignorant: it means that they are in denial.

No group of white women understood the differences in their status and that of black women more than the group of politically conscious white females who were active in civil rights struggle. Diaries and memoirs of this period in American history written by white women document this knowledge. Yet many of these individuals moved from civil rights into women's liberation and spearheaded a feminist movement where they suppressed and denied the awareness of difference they had seen and heard articulated firsthand in civil rights struggle. Just because they participated in antiracist struggle did not mean that they had divested of white supremacy, of notions that they were superior to black females, more informed, better educated, more suited to "lead" a movement.

In many ways they were following in the footsteps of their abolitionist ancestors who had demanded that everyone (white women and black people) be given the right to vote, but, when faced with the possibility that black males might gain the right to vote while they were denied it on the basis of gender, they chose to ally themselves with men, uniting under the rubric of white supremacy. Contemporary white females witnessing the militant demand for more rights for black people chose that moment to demand more rights for themselves. Some of these individuals claim that it was working on behalf of civil rights that made them aware of sexism and sexist oppression. Yet if this was the whole picture one might think their newfound political awareness of difference would have carried over into the way they theorized contemporary feminist movement.

They entered the movement erasing and denying difference, not playing race alongside gender, but eliminating race from the picture. Foregrounding gender meant that white women could take center stage, could claim the movement as theirs, even as they called on all women to join. The utopian vision of sisterhood evoked in a feminist movement that initially did not take racial difference or antiracist struggle seriously did not capture the imagination of most black women/women of color. Individual black women who were active in the movement from its inception for the most part stayed in their place. When the feminist movement began racial integration was still rare. Many black people were learning how to interact with whites on the basis of being peers for the first time in their lives. No wonder individual black women choosing feminism were reluctant to introduce their awareness of race. It must have felt so awesome to have white women evoke sisterhood in a world where they had mainly experienced white women as exploiters and oppressors.

A younger generation of black females/women of color in the late '70s and early '80s challenged white female racism. Unlike our older black women allies we had for the most part been educated in predominantly white settings. Most of us had never been in a sub-

ordinated position in relation to a white female. Most of us had not
been in the workforce. We had never been in our place. We were
better positioned to critique racism and white supremacy within
the women's movement. Individual white women who had attempted to organize the movement around the banner of common
oppression evoking the notion that women constituted a sexual
class/caste were the most reluctant to acknowledge differences
among women, differences that overshadowed all the common experiences female shared. Race was the most obvious difference.

In the '70s I wrote the first draft of *Ain't I a Woman: Black
Women and Feminism.* I was 19 years old. I had never worked a
full-time job. I had come from a racially segregated small town in
the south to Stanford University. While I had grown up resisting
patriarchal thinking, college was the place where I embraced feminist politics. It was there as the only black female present in feminist classrooms, in consciousness-raising, that I began to engage
race and gender theoretically. It was there that I began to demand
recognition of the way in which racist biases were shaping feminist
thinking and call for change. At other locations individual black
women/women of color were making the same critique.

In those days white women who were unwilling to face the reality of racism and racial difference accused us of being traitors by
introducing race. Wrongly they saw us as deflecting focus away
from gender. In reality, we were demanding that we look at the status of females realistically, and that realistic understanding serve as
the foundation for a real feminist politic. Our intent was not to diminish the vision of sisterhood. We sought to put in place a concrete
politics of solidarity that would make genuine sisterhood possible.
We knew that there could no real sisterhood between white
women and women of color if white women were not able to divest of white supremacy, if feminist movement were not fundamentally antiracist.

Critical interventions around race did not destroy the women's
movement; it became stronger. Breaking through denial about race
helped women face the reality of difference on all levels. And we
were finally putting in place a movement that did not place the class
interests of privileged women, especially white women, over that

of all other women. We put in place a vision of sisterhood where all our realities could be spoken. There has been no contemporary movement for social justice where individual participants engaged in the dialectical exchange that occurred among feminist thinkers about race which led to the rethinking of much feminist theory and practice. The fact that participants in the feminist movement could face critique and challenge while still remaining wholeheartedly committed to a vision of justice, of liberation, is a testament to the movement's strength and power. It shows us that no matter how misguided feminist thinkers have been in the past, the will to change, the will to create the context for struggle and liberation, remains stronger than the need to hold on to wrong beliefs and assumptions.

For years I witnessed the reluctance of white feminist thinkers to acknowledge the importance of race. I witnessed their refusal to divest of white supremacy, their unwillingness to acknowledge that an antiracist feminist movement was the only political foundation that would make sisterhood be a reality. And I witnessed the revolution in consciousness that occurred as individual women began to break free of denial, to break free of white supremacist thinking. These awesome changes restore my faith in feminist movement and strengthen the solidarity I feel towards all women.

Overall feminist thinking and feminist theory have benefitted from all critical interventions on the issue of race. The only problematic arena has been that of translating theory into practice. While individual white women have incorporated an analysis of race into much feminist scholarship, these insights have not had as much impact on the day to day relations between white women and women of color. Antiracist interactions between women are difficult in a society that remains racially segregated. Despite diverse work settings a vast majority of folks still socialize only with people of their own group. Racism and sexism combined create harmful barriers between women. So far feminist strategies to change this have not been very useful.

Individual white women and women of color who have worked through difficulties to make the space where bonds of love and political solidarity can emerge need to share the methods and strategies that we have successfully employed. Almost no attention is given the relationship between girls of different races. Biased feminist scholarship which attempts to show that white girls are somehow more vulnerable to sexist conditioning than girls of color simply perpetuates the white supremacist assumption that white females require and deserve more attention to their concerns and ills than other groups. Indeed while girls of color may express different behavior than their white counterparts they are not only internalizing sexist conditioning, they are far more likely to be victimized by sexism in ways that are irreparable.

Feminist movement, especially the work of visionary black activists, paved the way for a reconsideration of race and racism that has had positive impact on our society as a whole. Rarely do mainstream social critiques acknowledge this fact. As a feminist theorist who has written extensively about the issue of race and racism within feminist movement, I know that there remains much that needs to be challenged and changed, but it is equally important to celebrate the enormous changes that have occurred. That celebration, understanding our triumphs and using them as models, means that they can become the sound foundation for the building of a mass-based antiracist feminist movement.

Chapter 7

Resting in Gardens, Battling in Deserts

Black Women's Activism

Joy James

A version of this essay appeared in the Winter, 1999 issue of *Black Scholar*.

Reminding you
Sister
It's okay to rest your feet
from battles
But lay in gardens
warmed by sun
Not in spreading deserts
near convenient wells
—Audre Lorde

This epigraph is taken from an inscription by Audre Lorde for *The Black Unicorn*.[1] Lorde is one of many Black women writers, including Toni Cade Bambara, Sonia Sanchez, and Alice Walker, who have greatly influenced the growth and development, the genius, if you will, of womanist or Black feminist theory and activism.

Tens of thousands of Black women have furthered democratic politics and social justice through their activism and analyses. Black feminist politics displays a radical singularity. In its revolutionary tendency, only one of many trajectories within Black women's activism, one finds the framework for an alternative to liberal anti-racist and feminist politics. Black women have tended incredible, secluded gardens within the expansive wasteland of this dysfunctional democracy.

Depoliticizing representations often distract attention from the fruits of Black women's labors, obscuring their contributions to democratic politics. Often, commercial and stereotypical portrayals of Black females center on fetish and animalized sexual imagery; consequently, Blacks, females, and politics become effaced or distorted.

Racial and sexual caricatures corseting the Black female body have a strong historical legacy. Progressive intellectuals and activists satirize denigrating stereotypes that recycle vilifying images of Black females as tragic mulattas, tricksters, and femmes fatales. Nevertheless, commercial images of America's sexualized allure to or aversion for Black females eclipse images of Black female political agency in conventional culture. Deconstructing representations of Black females as sexual deviants, images that promote anti-Black and antifemale contempt and violence have been a primary concern of Black women writers and activists in the United States for centuries.

The political agency of Black women still seems to be infrequently referenced, perhaps because Black males remain the most influential petitioners and pugilists in contemporary American race politics. (Their ideological span stretches from the anti-civil rights activism of California's anti-affirmative action czar, Ward Connerly and Supreme Court Justice Clarence Thomas to the neo-radicalism of select black academics.) Although exceptions were made for extraordinary women, historically, recognized "freedom fighters" have been masculinized, a fact that furthers the erasure of Black women activists.

Historical Legacies

[W]e find our origins in the historical reality of Afro-American women's continuous life-and-death struggle for survival and liberation. Black women's extremely negative relationship to the American political system (a system of white male rule) has always been determined by our membership in two oppressed racial and sexual castes.... Black women have always embodied, if only in their physical manifestation, an adversary stance to white male rule and have actively resisted its inroads upon them and their communities in both dramatic and subtle ways.

—The Combahee River Collective[2]

The search for antiracist and feminist community can be measured by the heroic efforts of activist or ancestral African American women. Most Americans are unfamiliar with the history of militant Black female fighters, yet their stories are readily available. Memoirs such as *Crusade for Justice: The Autobiography of Ida B. Wells*; *Angela Davis: An Autobiography*; and *Assata: An Autobiography* touch a raw nerve among those who become politically stressed or polarized when facing radical and revolutionary social justice battles.[3] Paradoxically, political autobiographies expand an intellectual base for progressive struggles while simultaneously providing a comfort zone that validates images of revolutionaries marketed as commodities through publications for consumers.

Reading such autobiographies reveals rebellions that democratized American politics. Tens of thousands were and are inspired by Ida B. Wells' crusade against lynching, Ella Baker's organizing for civil rights, Angela Davis' support for prisoners (beginning with the Soledad Brothers in the late 1960s), and Assata Shakur's revolutionary battles in the Black Liberation movement (a movement eventually destroyed by the Federal Bureau of Investigation's illegal counterrevolutionary program, COINTELPRO). The works of women such as Wells, Baker, Davis, and Shakur—although not uniformly "radical" or "revolutionary," and with contradictions—pushed beyond conventional politics. Seeking liberation, each offered models of Black female resistance to political, social, state, or gender dominance.

Following the unique limbos, or political maneuvers, executed by Wells and Baker at the turn of the previous century, African American women continuously organized and shaped liberation leadership, leaving significant imprints on the movements of the

1960s and 1970s, although they were scarcely noted in conventional politics.

Black women who uniformly considered themselves "antiracists" but not necessarily "feminists" nevertheless expanded antiracist women's politics, community development, democratic power, and radical leadership. Given the primacy of movements in the formation and articulation of Black female militancy, history plays a central role in contemporary analyses. In the 1960s, Black women participated in the Southern Christian Leadership Conference (SCLC), the Student Nonviolent Coordinating Committee (SNCC), the Congress of Racial Equality (CORE), the Organization of Afro-American Unity (OAU), and the Black Panther Party.

Emerging from the Black Liberation and antiracist movements that helped to redefine radical action, in the 1970s, Black women's organizations such as the Combahee River Collective issued cogent manifestoes that articulated a revolutionary Black feminism.[4] Reviewing radical and revolutionary politics for contemporary struggles, we see legacies alive and changing in the activism of prisoners' rights advocates and environmental organizers. At a time of mass, militant unrest, through bold confrontations with state authority, Black women activists forged prototypes for late twentieth century, and early twenty-first century, Black female radicalism.

Of the many branches of Black feminisms extending from battles for a liberated African and female existence in America, the most imaginative and transformative take root in Black female radicalism. It is impossible here to offer a comprehensive survey of the ideological diversity or plurality of Black feminist activisms, or the more subtle differences found even within radical Black feminism. Yet it is essential that we examine the limits of liberalism or civil rights advocacy, as well as Black women's challenges to state power and antiradicalism within conventional feminist and antiracist politics.

The most recognized political activism remains in conventional politics. Despite exclusionary practices set by racism, sexism, and class bias, African American women have made gains in the "public realm" of electoral politics and appointed office; these are the political victories most often seen and celebrated in antiracist feminist politics. The 1992 election of Carol Mosley Braun as the United States' first Black woman senator (whose politics often fell short of progressive), and the reelections of Democratic leaders Maxine Waters (who helped to popularize the connections between the Central Intelligence Agency [CIA] and cocaine trafficking), Cynthia McKinney (active in human rights advocacy in US foreign policy), Corrine Brown, Carrie Meeks, and Eleanor Holmes Norton to the US House of Representatives, stand as key examples of Black female progress in electoral political power.

Outside of congressional halls, Black women also have mobilized the "private realm" of local and religious communities, neighborhood schools, and cultural centers. Directly or indirectly opposing institutional control, and social and state neglect or violence, they have informed American political culture by leaving indelible marks in antiviolence campaigns, resource redistribution for underresourced communities, youth and women's groups, and labor and civil rights activism. Both the highly visible congresswomen and the nearly invisible community activists shape models of political progressivism. Yet Black women activists and feminists are not uniformly progressive, although they all invariably face marginalization and opposition fueled by white supremacy, corporate capitalism, patriarchy, and homophobia. Radical or revolutionary Black feminism also faces resistance from liberal and conservative feminisms and antiracism. Black feminist politics negotiates the "internal" opposition of antiradicalism among feminists and antiracists and the counterfeminism evident among radicals.

Battling with state power and patriarchal culture, as well as antiradicalism and counterfeminism among progressives, subordinate women have forged a feminist politics through militant antiracist movements. Discomfort with Black feminist speech and activism in its most radical expressions—that which confronts exploitation tied to militarism, corporate dominance, and neoimperialism—stems from and fosters restricted notions of "feminism" and "antiracism." Difficulties in accepting Black feminisms on their own terms may stem from not only sexism and racism but also a lack of familiarity with critiques of monopoly capitalism and neoliberalism.

Given our economic and ideological diversity, we cannot in good faith posit Black women as a class. A homogenized view of women of African descent allows conventional politics to elide historical Black militancy. There is no "master" narrative that frames the concerns of all Black women and their organizations. The multiplicity of ideologies reveals varying degrees of political efficacy and risk for social change; this diversity is often obscured by the "framing" of feminism in ways that either erase the contributions of radical Black women or depict a homogeneous Black feminism as a (corrective or rebellious) appendage to either antiracist or feminist struggles. Resistance has historically challenged and shaped Black female praxis across a broad ideological spectrum. Black women's autonomy from the pervasive dominance of neoliberalism and corporate culture, however, opens new avenues for political activism.

Contemporary Black Feminism

Today, Black women's struggles center on related but seemingly diverse issues, such as reproductive rights, environmental racism, childcare and health issues, sexual violence, police brutality, and incarceration. Key intersections along the American political curve of antiracist, feminist activism include community, ideology and identity, revolutionary iconography, state punishment, sexuality, Black male patriarchy and profeminism, economic resources, and social and racial justice.

One area for concentrated focus has been the assault on affirmative action and the expansion of the prison industrial complex, combined, a twinned hydra for racial, economic, and gender repression. A resurgent neoconservatism hostile to "racial preferences" for education and employment acquiesces to racial bias in imprisonment and state execution. Of the nearly two million incarcerated in US jails, prisons, and detention centers, over 70 percent are people of color. The Washington, DC-based Sentencing Project has noted that Blacks convicted of committing similar offenses as whites are eight times more likely to be incarcerated.

Black women are increasingly becoming active around human rights abuses tied to policing and imprisonment, given the destructive impact official and unofficial policies have for their families and themselves. A few striking examples illustrate the gross inequality and abuse rampant in the prison industry and state policing: the Thirteenth Amendment to the Constitution legalizes slavery for prisoners; anyone convicted of killing a white person is four times more likely to receive the death penalty, particularly if she or he is not white; over 65 percent of juvenile offenders sentenced to death since the reinstitution of the death penalty in 1976 have been either Black or Latino. One of the few democratic nations to execute minors, the United States has executed more youths than any other country.[5]

Although they are a minority of the prison population, women, particularly women of color, are increasingly facing the punitive powers of the state. In March 1999, Amnesty International's Rights for All campaign issued a report, "Not Part of My Sentence: Violations of the Human Rights of Women in Custody," documenting the abuses of women in US prisons and jails. By June 1997, there were 138,000 women incarcerated in the United States, triple the number since 1985 and 10 times the number of women imprisoned in Spain, England, France, Scotland, Germany, and Italy combined.[6]

Most of the women incarcerated in the United States are nonviolent offenders convicted of economic crimes or drug use. Eighty percent are mothers, 80 percent are poor, and the majority are women of color. The less common violent offenses are generally connected to domestic violence. Racial bias in sentencing means that women of color incarcerated for nonviolent and violent crimes will increasingly make up the growing population of incarcerated females. Serving time, this population of caged women find themselves subject to new forms of physical and sexual abuse, and, although the Convention Against Torture, which the United States ratified in 1994, defines rape of women in custody by a correctional officer as torture, the United States government has engaged in virtually no monitoring of the conditions and situations of imprisoned women in respect to human rights violations.[7]

In theory, human rights protections exist for prisoners and nonprisoners in the United States under the International Covenant on Civil and Political Rights and the international convention's ban on racial discrimination, torture, and ill treatment. However, the government places itself above the law. In 1998, the United States continued to exempt itself from international human rights obligations that granted protections to US residents/citizens currently not available under US law. Even after ratification of key human rights treaties (generally the state weakens such treaties with reservations), the United States failed to acknowledge human rights law. It refused to ratify the international children's rights convention; opposed human rights initiatives banning landmines and child soldiers; and undermined the International Criminal Court (ICC). At the Rome Diplomatic Conference in July 1999, 120 states voted for and seven, including the United States, against the ICC treaty.[8] The above are only some of the battles which today's progressive activists face.

Conscious of both US domestic and foreign policies, Black women also continue to organize and theorize around other crises and conditions that erode freedom, democratic culture, and destroy life: racial and homophobic lynchings; the international AIDS epidemic currently devastating parts of Africa and US cities; refugees and regional wars; embargoes crippling Cuba and killing hundreds of thousands of Iraqi children; decolonization struggles in Puerto Rico and Ireland; Palestinian statehood; political prisoners in China and other countries as well as in the United States (which has over 100 political prisoners but only one on death row, Mumia Abu-Jamal); the war on drugs; addictions; the international resurgence of neo-Nazis; nuclear waste and toxic dumping; incest, rape, and domestic violence; underweight babies and infant mortality; dire poverty amid the increasing stratification of wealth; and, of course, hypertension and high blood pressure.

Conclusion

In a culture that greets anti-Black and antifemale violence, and the vilification and abuse of Black females and their kin with considerable equanimity, many are compelled to act. Some African

American women do so with distinct political intent to revolutionize rather than reform existing power structures, hoping to go to the root, to nurture and grow structural change that alleviates and diminishes oppressive conditions. Although for most Americans, the recognized public fighters or advocates remain male, the others, Black female organizers, battle as outsiders, at times criminalized as cultural and political outlaws. In these struggles, activists find that on one hand, the state has the power to extinguish a radical movement; on the other hand, it can modify and elevate that movement into the mainstream, so that it no longer functions as resistance to official policy. Sometimes the most convenient resting place seems to be in apolitical pursuits or politics that fit within conventional frameworks; some retreat into isolationist politics of their singular, pressing cause, abstracted from other struggles which could provide important tributaries for growth and development.

What we expect and demand of ourselves, society, and the state may fall short of our abilities to rethink and effectively counter corporate globalization, the stratification of wealth and poverty, the inhumane routinization of war (whether through bombing or embargo), and the increase of police powers (through the nefarious war on drugs and President Clinton's 1996 Omnibus Crime Bill).

Despite the institutional force and pervasive presence of state and corporate policies, Black feminist activism, like other insurgent action, reveals in its organizing and analyses its own peculiar power. Nowhere is this more evident than in the revolutionary potential of Black feminism found among the women of Jericho 98, the Black Radical Congress, and the prison and death penalty abolitionist movements, of activists who take rest and respite—just not by convenient wells.

1   This epigram is an excerpt from an inscription written by Audre Lorde to
    the author in September 1989 in the collection of poems, Audre Lorde, *The
    Black Unicorn* (New York: W. W. Norton, 1978).

2   Combahee River Collective, "The Combahee River Collective Statement,"
    in Gloria Hull, Patricia Bell Scott, and Barbara Smith (eds)., *All the Women
    Are White, All the Blacks Are Men, But Some of Us Are Brave: Black Women's
    Studies* (Old Westbury, NY: The Feminist Press, 1982).

3   Ida B. Wells, *Crusade for Justice: the Autobiography of Ida B. Wells,* Alfreda M.
    Duster (ed.), (Chicago: University of Chicago Press, 1970); Angela Davis,
    Angela Davis: An Autobiography (New York: Random House, 1974); Assata
    Shakur, *Assata: An Autobiography* (Westport, CT: Lawrence Hill & Co.,
    1987).

4   For anthologies documenting the emergence of Black feminist activism,
    see: Beverly Guy-Sheftall (ed.), *Words of Fire: An Anthology of
    African-American Feminist Thought* (New York: The New Press, 1995); Toni
    Cade Bambara (ed.), *The Black Woman* (New York: New American Library,
    1970); and Barbara Smith (ed.), *Home Girls: A Black Feminist Anthology* (New
    York: Kitchen Table: Women of Color Press, 1983).

5   The United States was to submit a report on its compliance with the
    Convention Against Torture in 1995 but no report has been released to
    date. In response, a coalition of over 60 nongovernmental organizations
    (NGOs) issued a report in October 1998 titled *Torture in the United States: The
    Status of Compliance by the U.S. Government with the International Convention
    Against Torture and Other Cruel, Inhuman or Degrading Treatment or Punishment.*
    See Morton Sklar (ed.), *Torture in the United States* (Washington, D.C.: World
    Organization Against Torture, October 1998). The report notes that the
    major areas of noncompliance in the United States center on: the death
    penalty; prison conditions and the treatment of refugee detainees; physical
    and sexual abuse of women in prisons; and the return of refugees to
    situations of torture and persecution and their long-term detention under
    abusive conditions. Other violations noted in the report are: the United
    States' failure to extradite or prosecute torturers who worked with the
    Central Intelligence Agency or were trained at the School of the Americas,
    the states' lack of adequate domestic implementation of the 1996 Illegal
    Immigration and Immigrant Responsibility Act; and arms sales and other
    assistance by the US government that support torture in foreign countries
    (such as the sale of electronic stun gun equipment and some 10,000 shock
    batons to Turkey to be used against the Kurdish minority, the same
    equipment which Amnesty International has denounced in its use against
    US prisoners).

6   Amnesty International, Rights for All, *Not Part of My Sentence: Violations of the
    Human Rights of Women in Custody* (New York: Amnesty International, March
    1999), 15-16. Amnesty documents that these European countries
    combined have a population of 150 million women as compared to 120
    million women in the United States.

7   See Sklar, *Torture,* 5.

8 See the 1999 Human Rights Watch Report published on the Black Radical Congress website: www.hrw.org/worldreport99/

Chapter 8

Riffin' on Music and Language

Amiri Baraka

This essay is based on a speech given at Naropa University in Boulder, Colorado in July 2000.

There's an essay that I put in this magazine called *Presidia 9* called "Doc Iment," for a poet who died in 1999 who was a close friend of mine, Gaston Neal. What is this document about? It's about word music, as we call it. Word music is poetry and music. It begins, "Doc I meant. What I say? Document?" Djali. That's the African word for what people call griot, which is a French word. Griot means "cry." Djali, on the other hand, does not mean to cry, but "to promote laughter." It's like a geo-socio aesthetic portrait of the world, which would be, for instance, the masks of theater, one is smiling, one is frowning. You have a geo-social aesthetic.

In college they taught us that the highest form of art is tragedy. Meaning Aeschylus, Sophocles, the dude that killed his father, slept with his mama, put out his own eyes, and searched the world for mediocrity. That dude. That's the first Crazy Eddie, Oedipus. What does Oedipus mean? Come on, Greek scholars, if you haven't had any Greek scholarship, you haven't been to school. It means "lame, clubfoot." Even today in urban America, corny people are called lame. Are we talking about Oedipus when we say "lame motherfucker"? Are we talking about language...about image or about history?

Afro-Americans are urban people, because as quiet as it's kept—independent of Jesse Helms and the rest of the people who want to make the world safe for nobody—the world is mixed, inalterably, ineffably mixed. If Africans were the first persons here, if you don't have some African trace in you, you must be from beyond the Van Allen Belt. In which case we would have to bring you in and spray you for some kind of weird disease.

Language, which began in one base and spread wherever the conditions had changed, is the oldest record of human life. These hands were once paws, all shaped the same way, and everybody read the same information down there on the ground. There wasn't much to see on the ground. Then there was the monkey who had to leap off the ground and therefore break his thumb, break his hand to turn it this way so that therefore I can pick up a stick and beat you to death, or a tool-making instrument.

At the same time, if you read Engels, is there anybody here who's not addicted to imperialism that would read Engels? Solid. He talks about the development of the hand as a form of labor, of society as a form of labor. We keep jumping up. You can't jump up with a paw. The woman said, "Why are you down here on the ground with these big-teeth animals? Why don't you get your lazy ass up off the ground? Get up?" So belatedly, he stood up and said, "I can't get that. My paw won't get it." Engels talks about the development of the vowels at the same time that the fingers developed. He talks about the development of a-e-i-o-u, the vowels; at the same time that's traced to the pentatonic scale. You're talking about music, about language, about anthropology. So that at the same time it becomes possible for you to not be cheetah to pick it up. With that kind of articulation, it becomes possible for you to say, ah, eh, ii, oh, uu. That is the beginning of language.

It means a lot of things. First, if you read Paul Robeson, does anyone know Paul Robeson's work, not his work as a singer, he was a great artist, but he was also an aesthetic theorist? His work on backgrounds of Afro-American music was very interesting and important. You can see that in his selected works. He talks about the pentatonic scale, the blues, the black notes. That's why the blues singers could play that easy, because they were the black notes.

But what Robeson said, and this was interesting, was that you can trace the development of the pentatonic, whether you're listening to the Volga boatmen in Russia and the Ukraine or Deep River in the South. It's essentially the same scale, the same chords. Robson goes through the whole technical, musical thing. I'd be glad to send the essay to you. If you can find the book, *Selected Writings of Paul Robson,* on Afro-American music, it's very important.

We talk about griot. Six o'clock and all's well, the town crier. The djali had a different function. It was literally to make you jolly. We get the term glee, glee man, glee club. When Louis Armstrong, for instance, used to sing, "Just because my hair is curly, just because my teeth are pearly, just because I wear a smile on my face all the time, that's why they call me Shine." We're talking about history that's not understood by those upon which it was shaped. We're walking around full of, "You square motherfuckers." Why do we say that? The Egyptians said square was the angle of failure. The pyramid was the angle of success. Who knows that on the street? We don't know that.

We talk about the griot vs. the djali. What is the djali's function? Griot is a word that comes into use through colonialism. If you go to Senegal, Mali, great places to go to, Ras, my second son, and I went there to visit the old slave castles. That's a hell of an experience. It's like the Jews when they go back to the concentration camps. It's something that breaks you down. We didn't say anything. I wrote my name inside an old castle. They said, "You mean there was a Baraka here many years ago?" But you know, when you see it, you go to the French possessions, you know, number one, nobody's there. You travel for miles, there's nobody in Senegal. You see the baobab trees and empty villages. Where are they? Maybe in Denver or LA or Oakland. But that strength of that French-African connection meant that the words coming out of Africa, like djali, would become griot. What is the job of the djali? Storyteller. That makes it abstract. Poet. Historian. Musician. Storyteller. Because if it's not a story, if it hasn't stored something, that's what a story is. It's a storage place. You store stuff in there. There's something interesting. So it's a historian.

The djali was supposed to go to each place and tell the history of the joint. Like Fidel Castro. When you go to Cuba, the first thing Fidel will do is tell you the whole history of the revolution. I mean in terms of a speech. From the beginning. In so-and-so we did so-and-so. Why? Because everybody is not up to speed on that. When the djali comes, the first thing they do is say, "You know the world begins and this happened. It used to be this. To get the point. And now this is the case."

Also, when the djali gets down you call that *djeliaw*. Billy Eckstein's most famous hit was "Jelly, Jelly, Jelly." There was a great pianist from New Orleans named Jelly Roll Morton. We always hook up jelly with sex. Why? You'll have to reason that out yourself. Must be jelly because jam don't shake like that. We could go on with these associations. Jam comes from *djama,* which means family, which ultimately means socialism, cooperative, *ujama.* So when he says, Jelly, Jelly, Jelly drove my old man crazy, made my mama wild. The point is that the djeliaw, their job is to light up the mind, to make the mind shine, to make the mind smile, to make the mind laugh, to make the mind laugh with understanding, recognition, to understand history as a revelatory story.

So that the poet, or at least the poet per my own self, like I said, Doc Iment, I'm not talking about what you might have meant, I'm talking about what I meant, the point is that for the *djali* the first function is to light up people's minds, to light up the understanding of the world. Why music? Because music is an expression of the word itself. In terms of why music, we're working on that now, when for instance you know the Greeks and Romans always used to say the Ethiopians were always smiling. This is a hell of a put-down because when you get down there with the sun picking stuff off the trees, which has a downside to it, it means people who wrest their life from the snow, who tended to be stricter, can come down and beat the shit out of you, ultimately, if you're not cool. There's an upside and a downside, an upside to the frown and a downside to the smile. Together it's infinity. You keep doing that and you keep going on. What we're trying to do is, human beings hopefully make a circle rather than always fluctuating. It's bound to have a dialectic to it. If there's an up there's a down. If there's a slow there's a fast. If there's a hot there's a cold. So where there was once the so-called masters of the universe, Egypt, the light of the world, they called themselves, who now must push bags for fat, aging businessmen. So there's an upside and a downside to everything.

Why music? Music is the motion of rising and changing, as thought given form, feeling as an object, the living reflection of material life, the thoughts I see, I hear, sonographics, drama itself. In terms of word music, the African, when we arrived here, now Afro-American, Black Americans, people who think that Africans remain Africans in the US are unrealistic. Duke Ellington, Thelonious Monk are Western musicians. When I taught at Yale with Bill Ferris, who's now the head of the National Endowment for the Humanities (NEH), we taught a course. He showed an incredible film. A drummer named Tony Williams, who used to play with Miles Davis, they took him to Africa to the shore. He comes to the shore of Africa and sets up his drum set and goes, boom, boom, pow, pow. A minute later they heard from across the way drums. The people are saying, "We heard you, but we don't understand what you're saying." Not only we heard you, but we heard you plural. Why plural? Because we play an industrial instrument. It's got levers. It's a little motor. They thought it was 10 or 15 people, when it was actually Tony Williams, you know, young Max Roach. There was a whole battalion of people. Why? Because that's an industrial, Western instrument, created by the one-man bands after the Civil War, the guys who stand out there, they don't want to go do the work, pick cotton or whatnot, so instead they pick up instruments—everything, harmonicas, drums, banjos, and started playing around with them. That's where that comes from, that is, to play it all.

The point is that this has not got to do with just the African qua nationality but the culture, which is now embedded in the US. If you don't think the American culture is African, European, and native, you don't know what you're talking about. That's what this whole idea is about Standard English. Hey, Americans never spoke English. Or about Ebonics. All of those are off the wall. Language is created by the people together. You cannot be on the West Coast and not speak Spanish. You know that. I want to go to Los Angeles. What are you going to say? You want to go to San Diego, what are you going to call it? You can't be in the Midwest unless you can speak Native American. You can't be in the South and not speak Bantu. There are more Bantu names, African names, in South Carolina, where they're trying to keep the flag up, which is why they're trying to keep the Confederate flag up. Because they figured all those Bantu names are going to rise up off the ground and get them.

You cannot speak an American sentence without going from Europe to Native America to Africa. We're one people. Even though the social thing keeps us separated and sometimes hateful and not understanding each other, we're still one people. A wild, wild thing. We have the history to kill each other off or to learn to be human beings. That's the way it is. Somebody told me that a long, long, long time ago and I said, Fiddlesticks. I didn't understand that then.

The question of word music. Music is a strictly abstract function, but music as a form of actual telling, for instance, "Meet me tomorrow at seven o'clock. Bring your largest knife and do not be late." At that point, where that is stopped, that is, take the drums away, why take the drums away, is it because you don't like percussion in your symphony orchestras? Why isn't there percussion in Europe? We have to ask, Why is the piano segregated? The question of history and art is the same thing. What happens in social history happens in aesthetic history, in arts. So if somebody suddenly says, "Look, boss, if you take that piece of wood away from them slaves, that wood they keep beating on, if you take that wood, all that notion about them rising up into the night, that would be over with." Fiddlesticks. Certainly that can't be true. How can that piece of wood be related to slave uprisings? Watch them, and for three more pork chops I will tell you.

Sure enough, that night, there he goes again. He hears it and says, "Ali, there is some kind of relationship. What is it?" "They're speaking to each other, boss." "You mean it's code?" "No, it's not a code. It's a language." "How can it be a language when they're just beating on the drum?" "Because it's a tonal language and they're using the drum under their arm, we call it the dundun, the drum shaped like the hourglass with the cords around it that you have with the drumstick shaped like a staff and you hold it under your arm like that so that you could make it like a stringed instrument, tight high, loose low. It's a tonal language. They're actually speaking to each other."

Why is that so important? The greatest drummers now are still playing a form of abstract expressionism. That is, they say, "We hear you, but we no longer understand what you're talking about, and neither do you!" You understand the emotion, which drives you and makes you do certain things, but to actually be able to say, "Meet me tomorrow."

In periods of backwardness such as the one we're in today, notice for instance how the music has changed. In the sixties, the rhythm and blues, the pop, very clear. There's no clearer singer, for instance, than the Motown people in terms of their words. You hear everything they say. Listen to Stevie Wonder. Marvin Gaye. They're clear. But then rap, I defy you to understand most of it just right off the thing. Reggae. Nobody clearer than Bob Marley. "Redemption Song." Tell me what they're singing now. Why is that? Because it is the society itself that no longer wants that clarity. When rap began, hip hop, and I say rap because it relates to the drum, that's what the sailors did on a log. What did the log do? It told what happened. That's the same thing.

What we're working on now in Newark is we have some groups called Blues People, which my wife and I have been running for about 15 years. We have poetry and music and drama the last Saturday of every month at our house in the basement. We have a 60-seat theater. We have a park. We do two things. If you're ever in that area, last Saturday of the month, four in the afternoon, we do a thing in Weequahic Park. It's about five bucks. Why are we doing that? Because you cannot allow the institutions created by imperialism to be the only purveyors of culture.

You cannot become merely a passive receiver of culture. You cannot in the meantime be a dog in the manger and trying to wait until imperialism discovers you. A lot of people say, I'm out here being this and that, but as soon as el hombre discovers you, you turn into a ho, whore. They'll turn you into what they are.

It's the job of people who think of themselves as advanced or progressive to create a living culture themselves. Even Naropa...what would this whole scene here be without this alternative institution? We need these in every city. Where Black people live as plurality, majority, that's 27 cities. The biggest cities in the US. We need a network. Why should we go to all those jazz festivals in Europe? Sure, we're going to go to them, why not? But why should those be the only things we attend? Where's the Zimbabwe jazz festival, the Beijing jazz festival? Where is the Pyongyang jazz festival, the Ho Chi Minh City jazz festival? It sounds like I'm a communist, and it's true.

Why do we limit ourselves to the things constructed by the people that oppress us? And if you don't think you're oppressed, then you're oppressed past recognition. That question is important. How can we extend the role and the value of poetry? Another thing is a Newark music project in which we do all the music of the people in the city and the state. In Newark we did Sarah Vaughan, who was born there, Babs Gonzales, Willie "the Lion" Smith, Wayne Shorter. Why? Because each one of those cities has a history of a culture that is multinational. We have put together a thing called the Newark, New Jersey store. Everybody from Stephen Crane to Allen Ginsberg. Both Allen and I were born in Newark. We've got William Carlos Williams, too, because Paterson's right up the street. Stephen Crane and Sarah Vaughan, and Joe Pesci and Jerry Lewis. With that kind of mix you can't go wrong. Every city in the US has that mix. If you were to do a history of Denver or Boulder and Colorado you'd find out some things that would amaze you. Like last week when George Segal and Jake Lawrence died. They had Segal on the front page of the *Newark Star Ledger*, which is a racist newspaper. New Jersey artist, but Segal was not from New Jersey. Jake Lawrence is. They could have them both up there. The *Times* did have both of them up.

Why are we doing this? So that we can give the people of this city a way into history other than the one proposed for them. The last thing is the Lincoln Park Coast Culture District, which is to rebuild a certain part of our city. It turns out that the old abolitionist sector, where Lincoln visited, Newark, is the third-oldest city in the

US. So the old abolitionist district, where Lincoln visited, and the Black entertainment district, naturally are together. They're the last districts not taken over completely by imperialism. Why? Because they were slums. We have claimed them, although the gentleman told me he had been authorized by God to take all of this property back, but we're going to rebuild that. We're rebuilding the Kruger Scott mansion, Kruger, the beer baron, Scott is a hairdresser, a mansion to recreate the history of the people in that city. We're talking about a new kind of museum, not a museum of strange objects, but of people's wedding photos, the 1950s teams, who was the prettiest woman on Norfolk Street in 1938, who were the bandits of the north ward in 1920, what beer baron lived in these big mansions? That is to give a history of the place that actually places it in the place where people lived, not just as a receptacle for imperialist culture.

The last thing I mentioned is the thing that we're working on now, myself, personally, and some people are helping me, is that we're trying to reclaim word music. We have actually written music so that when we write words they correspond to notes. If you write b-a-t, that actually corresponds to a chord. These are things that we're working on so that for instance one day, and any of you poets who are interested in coming out there who are serious and revolutionary, because we're not doing this just to strum our own gourds, we're trying to create alternative means of communication and networking.

Chapter 9

How Ya' Like Me Now?

Rap and Hip Hop Come of Age

Yvonne Bynoe

> [H]ip-Hop is the world the slaveholders made, sent into
> nigga-fide future shock. Hip-Hop is the plunder from down un-
> der, mackin' all others for pleasure. Hip-Hop is the Black aes-
> thetic by-product of the American dream machine, our culture
> of consumption, and subliminal seduction...There is no such
> thing as good Hip-Hop or bad Hip-Hop, progressive Hip-Hop
> or reactionary Hip-Hop, politically incorrect Hip-Hop or
> Hip-Hop with a message. It's either Hip-Hop or it ain't. Shit.
>
> —Excerpt from "Definition of Hip-Hop," by Greg Tate
>
> This is rebellion music, not gangsta music.
>
> —KRS-One

In the words of rap artist Common, "One day it will all make
sense."[1] Perhaps in 50 years, we will have tributes to acknowledge the musical contributions of Public Enemy and maybe
Rakim will be recognized as an American cultural icon, but today many people are grappling to understand the relevance of
rap music and hip hop culture. Rap music—love it or hate it—is
a direct descendant of the African oral tradition. Black folks
have been rapping since the first African griot. Slaves were trad-
ing big lies and verbally abusing opponents in rhymes in what
was then known as *pattin' juba;* the musical accompaniment was
the rhythmic slapping of the chest and the thighs. *Pattin' juba*

evolved into the *dozens* and epic tales called *toasts*. It is from this oral tradition that modern rap was born. The majority of the toasts lionized mythical bad men such as Stagolee and tricksters like Shine. Stagolee was the ultimate outlaw. Tricksters like Shine, however, used wit and mental skills to outsmart white men and to get sex. Today's rap artists with their tales of sexual prowess, illegal empires, and their verbal battles are following in the tradition of the toasters who rapped about Stagolee and Shine and who played the dozens with their cronies on street corners.

Rap remains mired in controversy, however controversies regarding Black music and its artists are nothing new. African American music that came from the streets has always embarrassed the Black bourgeoisie class who wanted art to "uplift the race." During the Harlem Renaissance, this group disliked Negro spirituals, detested the blues, and hated the now-lionized jazz because it was too closely associated with the *demimonde*. The major distinction between that era and today is that then, in segregated America, Black people's dirty laundry was aired only among family; now in this age of global media, the entire world gets a peek. As such, the ashamed Black middle class is now being joined by frightened white suburbanites whose rebellious children are buying an estimated 70 percent of the rap music consumed in this country.[2]

Rap is American, but with a defiant shout. The sexism, violence, and nihilism that are depicted in rap music are a byproduct of that which exists in this country. Rap music, by its nature, is confrontational and at times vulgar, but these characteristics do not negate it as a true musical art form. Critics like jazz musician Delfayo Marsalis say that rap music is not art because art "transcends life" rather than imitates it.[3] Professor Maulana Karenga's definition of art, however, speaks to those who value realism, stating, ". . . cultural production informed by standards of creativity and beauty and inspired by and reflective of a people's life experiences and life aspirations."[4] Therefore, rap music is art because it validates the lives of people who live in the 'hood and also those who are invisible in society. As is the case with all art, not every rap song is a masterpiece or even particularly significant to the genre, but others are priceless.

Spike Lee, in his movie *Bamboozled*, slyly alludes to rap artists as being the equivalent of modern-day minstrels, a sentiment echoed by many Black Americans, including rap artist Chuck D. To an extent the critics are right; we have been bamboozled by the entertainment industry. Similar to the recruitment of Mantan and Eat n' Sleep to the New Millennium Minstrel show, annually a succession of young, undereducated Black men, seeking to escape dead-end jobs or the streets, are welcomed by the music industry. The record companies encourage these young people to tell their ghetto tales (real or imagined) in the crudest fashion for predominately white rap CD buyers. Right now, the most successful rap artists can become multimillionaires by being vulgar, misogynistic, and antisocial. More importantly, there are Black executives who are promoting this type of rap music to impressionable youth; Black video directors coming up with scurrilous video concepts; young Black women begging to disrobe for these videos; and a population of Black adults who by being silent are accomplices to this cultural hoodwinking. Critics, rather than solely blaming the rap artists, would be better served to address the corporate minstrel makers and the circumstances that produce willing coons: poverty, ghetto conditions, unemployment, and unequal opportunities.

If there is a problem within rap music and Hip Hop culture, it is a lack of diversity, rather than a need for censorship. The world of hip hop, like the rest of Black America, is not a monolith, yet all too often hip hop is only represented by young Black males, with gold teeth, wearing baggy pants, shouting obscenities, and libidinous young Black women shakin' their asses. What the music industry has done through rap music is to frame the "authentic" Black American, not as a complex, educated, or even creative individual, but as a "real nigga" who has ducked bullets, worked a triple beam, and who has done at least one bid in prison. This image, along with that of scantily clad women, is then transmitted worldwide as a testament of who Black Americans are. This means that corporate entertainment entities have no vested interest in seeing that rap artists advance themselves creatively or intellectually. The contrary is true, as W.E.B. Du Bois asserts in *Color and Democracy*, saying that colonizers' "sudden interest…in the preservation of native culture" and in their vernacular is a way to keep primitives from "modern cultural patterns."[5] In essence, if the media image of rap music and hip hop is radically altered, then the societal image of an "authentic" Black American would also have to be radically altered.

Unlike the early days of rap music, when all types of styles and messages coexisted, today corporate entertainment only allows one rap type at a time. With an extremely narrowed concept of rap, there has developed a schism within the hip hop community as to how it should be represented and by whom. Although it is a drastic oversimplification of the genre, for this brief discussion, there have developed essentially two camps of rap devotees: the ones who favor so-called "conscious rap," which caters to an underground audience, and those who favor the glitzy, "commercial rap" that is played incessantly on urban radio. These terms themselves are almost misnomers since a "conscious" artist can become "commercial," although the converse is rarely true. This was the case with "conscious" rap artist Lauryn Hill who became a "commercial" artist. In 1999, Hill became the first woman ever to win five Grammy awards in one year including "Album of the Year," for *The Miseducation of Lauryn Hill*; Hill had been nominated for 10 Grammys that year. Moreover, the terms are subjective since many of the "conscious" rap artists use profanity and the word nigga, smoke weed, and are unwed parents, and some "commercial" artists are reflective and produce thought-provoking work. At best, the terms are shorthand, with "conscious" meaning socially and politically aware and "commercial" meaning materialistic and libertine.

In 1987, Biz Markie's video for his song "The Vapors" was perhaps the first "lifestyle" rap video. The video took place on a large commercial boat sailing in what was probably New York harbor, with Big Daddy Kane, a few other heads, and a couple of women in fairly modest bathing suits. The 1990s version of that video would show Biz, an entourage, a sumptuous million-dollar home, a personal yacht, a bevy of thong-wearing women, and a stable of expensive cars. Although many critics state that "commercial" rap artists are apolitical, it could be argued that they support a free market economy. Many "commercial" rap entrepreneurs like Sean "Puffy" Combs (Bad Boy Entertainment), Jay-Z (Roc-a-Fella Entertainment), Master P (No Limit), Dr. Dre (Aftermath), and Jermaine Dupri (So So Def), as well as a host of artists such as Lil' Kim, Foxy Brown, and Cash Money Millionaires, are unapologetically capitalists, equating the struggle for equality with the ability to get paid. Their rationale is that America is a capitalist society that runs on money, thus those who have the money (regardless of how it's obtained) are those who rule. Their ethos is summed up by Lil' Kim in the song, "Money Power and Respect:" "First you get the money, then you get the power and then you get the mother fucking respect."[6] Although the concept seems to have worked for hip hop impresario Russell Simmons, most "commercial" rap artists never seem to advance beyond the "get the money" phase.

Driven by a need for self-aggrandizement, many Black hip hop millionaires are still comparing their power to that of their white peers. The comparison is useless, since the hip hop millionaires have not studied how power works or is used politically, preferring to imitate the style but not the substance of power. Moreover, hip hop millionaires are not substantively engaged in philanthropy, a route used by mogul David Geffen to extend his power far beyond the boundaries of the entertainment industry. The trial of multimillionaire Sean "Puffy" Combs, who was charged with gun possession and bribing a witness in connection with a nightclub shooting, proves that despite his money, he has gained neither power nor respect.

While "commercial" rap artists extol the virtues of conspicuous consumption, "conscious" rap artists discuss empowerment through politics and knowledge. Among those flying the flag of "conscious" hip hop is Common (Lonnie Rashid Lynn). With the release of his fourth album, titled *Like Water for Chocolate* (taken from the Mexican novel), Common has finally found mainstream success. Prior to the album's release Common was probably best known for his hats, being from Chicago, and his rap battle with former NWA member Ice Cube, which resulted in his retaliatory single, "For the Bitch in Yoo." Generally, Common's songs talk about gaining self-awareness in a society consumed by self-destructive principles. His topics have included abortion, the deceit of the music industry, sexual restraint, the Black family, and the direction of hip hop. On this latest album, Common includes tributes to Nigerian artist Fela Kuti and Assata Shakur, who he went to Cuba to meet. "A Song for Assata" recounts her capture by police and her exile to Cuba. Common may be "conscious" but he is not totally politically correct. He has been accused of homophobia for his use of the term faggot on his song, "Dooinit;" he denies the charge, but admits that he did use the term as a pejorative. Common, however, is the first to admit that he is evolving as a man and as an artist.

Mos Def (Dante Beze) is the current darling of the "conscious" hip hop world. The Brooklyn native and his partner Talib Kweli stepped into the forefront with the release of their album, *Mos Def and Talib Kweli Are . . . Black Star* in 1998. Called Marcus Garveyesque by some, this album provided desperate fans with a new source of smart rap music. A year later Mos released his solo album, *Black on Both Sides,* which was certified platinum. This album displayed not only Mos' versatility as a trained musician, but also his insightful Black power politics. Mos' activism, however, goes beyond rhyming. Reminiscent of KRS-One's "Stop the Violence" effort nearly a decade ago, Mos organized a collective of rap artists to record the *Hip Hop For Respect* CD and video. *Hip Hop For Respect* protested the shooting death in New York City of African immigrant Amadou Diallo by four policemen. The proceeds from the CD went to the Hip Hop For Respect Foundation, a nonprofit organization that encourages entertainment industry professionals to become involved in their fans' communities. To that end, Mos Def and Talib Kweli purchased Nkiru Books in Brooklyn, New York, which was on the verge of bankruptcy. Mos is also an actor and has appeared as a member of the Mau Maus rap group in the movie *Bamboozled;* in a VISA commercial; on an episode of the television show *NYPD Blue;* and in Suzan Lori-Parks' Pulitzer Prize winning play, *Top Dog/Underdog.* Like Lauryn Hill, Mos is a "conscious" rap artist poised to become "commercial."

The most political rap artists since Public Enemy may be the duo dead prez. Much of dead prez's lyrical influences come from the Black Power movement. Identifying with the history of Black political struggle is the core to the duo's philosophy. On their first album, *Let's Get Free,* many of the songs outline the overlooked history of the struggle of Black people, with the listener being urged to immediately get involved with progressive political projects. Challenging the hypocrisy of much rap music and hip hop culture, M-1 has been quoted as saying:

> Hip Hop today is programmed by the ruling class. It is not the voice of African or Latino or oppressed youth. It is a puppet voice for the ruling class, that tells us to act like those people who are oppressing us. Who's to blame? The schools, the media, capitalism, and colonialism are totally responsible for what Hip Hop is and what it has become. But we didn't intend on that— Hip Hop was a voice just like the drum, the oral tradition of our people.[7]

dead prez sees hip hop as a commodity in the world of global capitalism, but one that can have social value to people of color if artists are willing to retake control of it. The duo reconciled their business alliance with Loud Records by deeming it a strategic means of getting "their" message out to as many people as possible, thus being able to create more radicals.

Censorship is one of the evils that dead prez continues to fight. Rawkus Records deleted their verse for the *Hip Hop For Respect* CD. The duo's record company, Loud Records, chose to slap a sticker over the cover photo *Let's Get Free,* which shows youths in Soweto, guns held high, celebrating a victory over police. Additionally, video outlets such as Black Entertainment Television (BET) and Music Television (MTV) reportedly asked Loud Records to edit the video for dead prez's single, "They Schools." The clip in question blasts the US educational system for its miseducation of people of color with such no-nonsense images as the duo being hanged with nooses and the burning of textbooks. The artists have also been banned from several venues in New York because of their political messages.

Although individual artists and groups are political, a long-standing criticism of hip hop it that it has not generated a sustainable political movement. The criticism is somewhat illogical since overt political engagement was not hip hop's *raison d'etre*. Rap music began as community entertainment and any political function was largely subtextual or incidental. Before any large-scale movement can be contemplated, the post-civil rights generation would first have to build a viable political apparatus, just as the Black Arts Movement was the sister organization to the Black Power Movement. Hip hop is a cultural expression whereas politics is concerned with influencing governmental policy. The two purposes seem to be mutually exclusive, since hip hop seeks to define a specific group reality within our society, while politics seeks to define (or redefine) society at large. In basic terms, raising awareness about police brutality through a song or performance is rap/hip hop, but actually motivating the electorate to force changes in police department procedures and/or the laws used to prosecute corrupt cops is politics.

Rap music entered the overt political realm in 1982 when Grandmaster Flash and The Furious Five rapped about life in the ghetto on *The Message*. By the late 1980s, the commercial success of politically "conscious" rap artists had caused the media to identify them, rather than young activists, organizers, and legislators, as the political spokesmen of the hip hop generation. Unfortunately, the inability of these insightful artists to organize a political movement underscores the contradiction of so-called hip hop politics. If the hip hop community ever spawns a "movement" it will be because it galvanizes around a particular issue or set of issues that require legislative redress like the Bay Area's Third Eye Movement did in 1999 in its fight against Proposition 21. Moreover, in doing so, the participants would make clear distinctions between culture and politics. In this "movement" rap artists would use their celebrity to raise public awareness but full-time community organizers, activists, and emerging politicians would lead it.

Movements in large part depend on consensus, and currently, within the hip hop community there is still a debate as to the role of whites. Although they are the chief financial supporters of the genre, buying the vast majority of CDs, rap publications, and concert tickets, the music and culture remains heavily steeped in a

Black, urban aesthetic. Rap artists are still predominately Black and rap artists must still get love on the streets, before they can reach potential fans in suburbia. While some see rap music and hip hop as bridging the racial divide, there are other rap fans who are wary of white fans, especially those who embrace hip hop's most outré elements. In a 1999 interview Mos Def said,

> [T]hese kids in the suburbs that buy their first Wu Tang record and lose their damn mind—-they could play an active part in the culture if they wanted to, but that is not why they bought that Wu Tang record. They bought that Wu Tang record to live out their fantasy of themselves as Raekwon or Ghost or Method or whoever. A lot of hip hop nowadays seems like the primitive prototype for what virtual reality is going to be in the next few years—live somebody else's life feel somebody else's pain and frustration.[8]

Other Black fans are simply wondering whether rap music is on the verge of being hijacked by white interests the same way rock n' roll was in the 1950s.

White rap artist Eminem is the lightning rod for this latest rap debate. Like many rap artists before him, Eminem's lyrical content is objectionable, Black audiences like him, and he is associated with a rap veteran—Dr. Dre. However, unlike any Black rap artist to date, his second album, *The Marshall Mathers LP* has sold over eight million records; he has been heralded as a comic genius in the media; and his grossly crude tales have been nominated for an "Album of the Year" Grammy. Times certainly have changed since 1989, when three of the five nominated rap acts, including winner DJ Jazzy Jeff and the Fresh Prince, stayed home to protest the Grammys' decision to present the new "Best Rap Performance" award off-camera. The Grammys at that time were charged with being out of touch with popular culture. It is not clear whether giving Eminem an "Album of the Year" nomination is a sign of their hipness or their hypocrisy. The Grammys indicate that sales are not the sole determinant for a nomination. So what are the criteria asks writer Chic Smith,

> [I]f Eminem is not being nominated for his sales and his chart positions throughout 2000, what is the nomination for? Surely, NARAS is not endorsing his homophobic lyrics or his songs about murder and rape. From an artistic standpoint, perhaps NARAS appreciates the cleverness in which those derogatory messages are conveyed. Perhaps the Grammy awards are like the electoral process in America: in desperate need of reform.[9]

Maybe the Grammys like the rest of America, popular culture has simply gotten coarser and Eminem is reaping the benefits of lower standards. Possibly, but could it be that Eminem is the latest Great White Hope of corporate entertainment: an "angry blond" rapper? In the 1950s, to assuage parents uncomfortable with white kids, especially young white girls, bopping to Chuck Berry and Bo Diddley, Elvis was presented as a substitute: a white boy who sounded "Black." Elvis, because of his race, was then able to avail himself of financial and media opportunities at that time closed to Black artists. As a result, Elvis and not Berry or Diddley became known as the "King of Rock n' Roll." Similar racial politics allowed Paul Whiteman to be named the "King of Jazz" in the 1930s and Benny Goodman to be the "King of Swing" in the 1940s. Will Eminem be crowned the King of Rap? It's doubtful, but what is more important is determining whether rap music and hip hop culture represent a true cross-cultural exchange or are they just another victim in the fight for cultural dominance?

James Baldwin said, "To be conscious in America is to be in a constant state of rage." For those of us who are conscious, all of this is about more than hip hop. Hip hop is simply the metaphor for our lives. If our elders give up on hip hop, then they've given up on us. If we give up on hip hop, then we've given up on ourselves. Despite its dynamism, hip hop can be no more than what we are capable of saying or allow to be said.

1   Common, *One Day It'll All Make Sense*, Loud Records, 1997.

2   Charles Aaron, "Black Like Them," *Spin Magazine*, November 1998.

3   Delfayo Marsalis, "The Art of Rap?" *Elementary*, June-August 1996.

4   Maulana Karenga, *Introduction to Black Studies* (Los Angeles: University of Sankore Press, 1982). Also Maulana Karenga, *Kawaida Theory: An Introductory Outline* (Los Angeles: Kawaida Publications, 1980).

5   Ross Possnock, *Color and Culture: Black Writers and the Making of the Modern Intellectual* (Cambridge, MA: Harvard University Press, 1998), 91.

6   The Lox, featuring Lil' Kim and DMX, "Money, Power & Respect," on *Money, Power & Respect*, Bad Boy Entertainment, 1998.

7   Chas Walker, "Cultural Weaponry," *Colorlines* 4, no. 3 (Winter 2000-01).

8   Oliver Wang, "Midnight Sun," *San Francisco Bay Guardian*, 16 September 1998.

9   Chic Smith, "Will the Real Grammy Please Stand Up?" Urban Think Tank, Inc., February 2001, http://www.UrbanThinkTank.org.

Chapter 10

Mixed Signals

Race and the Media

Alice Tait and Todd Burroughs

We don't control our economics or education, our enforcement
or our environment. Then there's the tendency of not having
control over the realities, and that means the fantasy world can
be dealt and sold to us very easily. So people become what they
see, and when people become what they see, a reflection or a
limited reflection can end up as a direct interpretation.

–Chuck D, founder of Public Enemy[1]

On April Fool's Day, 2002, an email press release announced
that Black Entertainment Television (BET), long criticized
for appealing to the lowest common denominator, was
overhauling its schedule.

In what the release described as "major shifts" in network programming philosophy, network officials said BET would stop
showing music videos featuring images of overly sexualized Black
women and glamorized violence. The network was also creating a
new morning newsmagazine—a Black progressive version of *Good
Morning America* and *Today* called *Good Morning, Black America*.

Davey D, a well-known hip hop DJ and community activist in
California, signed the email and ended it with this line: "The following (sic) story is wishful thinking and fantasy gone astray . . . ."[2]

For anyone interested in the state of Black-owned media in the
US, the joke was painfully on target. It expressed community dis-
appointment with Black Entertainment Television (BET), which

was the largest Black-owned media company in America until 2000[3] and reaches 98 percent of the nation's Black cable subscribers.[4] (BET is now a subsidiary of the white media conglomerate Viacom.) And it might be argued that this "prank" laments the decline of local and national Black public affairs programming, especially in light of BET's shortcomings. It clearly illustrates the danger of trusting that black ownership or influence automatically guarantees fair and varied representation of the African American community.

Finally, the timing is also revealing. Increased emphasis on profit and rapid deregulation and conglomerization in the communication industry has created an especially difficult climate for African Americans interested—as producers or consumers—in socially conscious media.

Too Much Information?

Approximately 99 percent of Americans own televisions, 70 percent of whom subscribe to cable; 100 percent own radios; and 77 percent subscribe to newspapers. In most homes, the television set is on at least seven hours per day, though studies find children watch about eight hours a day. Americans listen to the radio 2.5 hours a day and spend 45 minutes reading their daily newspapers. In addition, Americans receive most of their news from television and often believe what they see and hear on the news.[5] African Americans watch and listen to more broadcast media than these averages. For example, African Americans spend more than 70 hours a week watching television—20 to 35 percent more than whites.[6]

The power of the media is profound. It sets agendas, interprets meaning, confers status, and in its worst case, endorses destructive behavior. It's most powerful impact is on children, who frame definitions of and draw conclusions about the world through the messages they receive. Studies conducted in the 1990s show that children across all races associate positive characteristics more with white characters they see on television, and negative characteristics with the minority characters. Although children believe that all races are shown doing both good and bad things on the news, they agree that the news media tend to portray both African American and Latino people more negatively than white or Asian individuals. African American children feel that entertainment media represent their race more fairly than the news media (47 percent to 25 percent). Asian children feel the opposite, favoring the news media (36 percent to 28 percent), while white and Latino children are split between the two. All ages and races expressed faith that the media could help bring people together by showing individuals of varying races interacting together.[7]

Yet as a capitalist enterprise, the main purpose of the Eurocentric media—media created by and reflecting the worldview of people of European descent— is to create and maintain consumers of all ages. And the Eurocentric media is experiencing steady growth and rapid consolidation. The top media corporations that have "dominant" power over American culture have shrunk to only ten.[8] Although one of them, AOL Time Warner, is now headed by Richard Parsons, a Black man, this top echelon is almost completely white. Not surprisingly, the product—whether packaged in magazines or television shows—is oriented toward a white audience.

Meanwhile, the Afrocentric media—media created by and reflecting the worldview of people of African descent—is generally struggling to keep afloat.

In Our Own Images

Afrocentricity involves a systematic exploration of relationships, social codes, cultural and commercial customs, mythoforms, oral traditions, and proverbs of the peoples of Africa. It is the belief in the centrality of Africans in modern history.

Since the founding of *Freedom's Journal*, the first African American newspaper in 1827, Blacks have attempted to create Afrocentric media—media that serve their various informational, educational, political, cultural, and spiritual needs.

Over the last four centuries, Blacks have created newspapers, journals, magazines, radio and television programs, and World Wide Web sites, yet such attempts have met with varying levels of success, particularly in the realm of broadcasting. Although representations of Blacks on television made notable gains in the 1970s, 1980s, and mid-1990s with a handful of dramatic series and situation comedies that featured African Americans, the medium seemed to usher in the millennium in retrogressive style.

Under the leadership of president Kweisi Mfume, the NAACP threatened to lead a boycott of the three major television networks when their 1999–2000 season lineups had no persons of color in leading roles. The boycott never materialized, but it brought to light the whiteness of television, with the exception of some cable efforts like HBO's *Boycott,* the story of a young Martin Luther King leading the Montgomery Bus Boycott, and Showtime's *Soul Food.*[9]

Nevertheless, the dream of Black television network ownership, although battered, still survives. Two new "mini-networks" are attempting to snip at BET's heels—New Urban Entertainment Television (NUE-TV) and the Major Broadcasting Corporation (MBC). Blacks are the primary partners in both enterprises. MBC—whose principal partners include singer Marlon Jackson and boxer Evander Holyfield—has made the most progress, with its signal now being carried on several major cable networks, including Comcast. MBC carries contemporary gospel videos, church services, classic 1970s made-for-television movies such as *The Autobiography of Miss Jane Pittman,* and Black college sports. NUE-TV's future is unclear, since no major cable carrier, at this writing, has agreed to carry its signal. The good news is that national Black syndication efforts, such as Frank Mercado-Valdes' Heritage Network (formerly called African Heritage Network), are thriving because they require sales to individual stations, not an entire channel.

Meanwhile, more obstacles to Black ownership and influence in broadcasting are emerging. Michael Powell, son of Colin Powell and the chairman of the Federal Communications Commission (FCC) under President George W. Bush, is actively pursing open deregulation of the broadcast industry, putting in jeopardy small Black-owned broadcasters who own single radio stations. These entrepreneurs were already hurt by the Telecommunications Act of 1996, which spurred merger-mania in the communication and media industries. Only Radio One, the Black media conglomerate owned by Cathy Hughes, continues to be a national "major player" in radio. Radio One, the largest Black-owned media company in America since the sale of BET, owns less than 100 radio stations.

There are some "stars" in radio, like nationally syndicated radio entertainment programs such as *The Tom Joyner Morning Show* and *The Doug Banks Show* which are targeted directly to African Americans. The shows feature political commentary and interviews with Black newsmakers. Joyner's show is syndicated by ABC Radio Networks, and led to the creation of *BlackAmericaWeb.com*, an online newspaper. Tavis Smiley—the founding host of *BET Tonight*) who appears on the Joyner show—is a nationally syndicated commentator on ABC radio, and hosts a syndicated National Public Radio program for an African American audience.

But these shows, with their wide reach, are the exceptions. The membership of the National Association of Black-Owned Broadcasters, the organization of Black-owned radio owners, totals less than 300 members in 2002.[10] This is in stark contrast to the conglomerates that own *hundreds* of radio stations around the nation.[11]

The Limitations of Public Affairs Programming

Like Black radio, Black public affairs television programs have also been a resource for Black viewers, but the changing climate is making it difficult for these shows to survive. These local programs, virtually all originally produced and conceived by white television executives after the urban disturbances of 1967 and 1968, began airing in major markets after King's assassination. By the 1970s, most major markets could boast one, if not several of these programs. The best known might be New York City's *Like It Is,* hosted by Gil Noble on WABC-TV.

Despite the audiences these local shows served, there have only been two national Black public affairs programs. *Black Journal* (1968–1970) was PBS's Black news magazine, and *Soul!* (1968–1973) which produced, and reproduced, a Black aesthetic. They originally aired on National Educational Television, the predecessor to the Public Broadcasting Service (PBS). *Black Journal* premiered in June 1968 and received critical acclaim and strong viewer response. But Bill Greaves, sole host of the show by 1970, left that year to focus on his film company. *Black Journal* did a nationwide search for a new producer/host. It decided on a colleague of Greaves', a Detroit civil rights activist named Tony Brown. With white commercial corporate sponsorship, Brown moved the show to commercial syndication in 1977, where it was renamed *Tony Brown's Journal.* Brown's own Tony Brown Productions produced it, and continues to do so today. But *Soul!,* a weekly Black art showcase, was a fixture of PBS for a shorter period of time—from 1968 to 1973. The more radical of the two programs, perhaps, *Soul!* featured Black artists at the height of the Black Power and Black Consciousness movements, which were designed to spiritually and psychologically reunite African Americans with their African heritage.

Though *Tony Brown's Journal* and two other national programs, *BET Tonight* and *America's Black Forum,* (the latter syndicated) are surviving, many of the local television programs are beginning to disappear. *Like It Is,* a 34-year-old Black public affairs program in New York City that has produced major Afrocentric documentaries on the civil rights and Black Power movements, has been threatened with extinction if it doesn't bring in advertising dollars to pay for itself. In 2001, *Urban Update,* a Black public affairs show in Boston, was canceled and subsequently reinstated—with a drastically smaller budget—after community protests.[12] And *The Bottom Line,* a public affairs program in Baltimore hosted by NAACP president Kweisi Mfume, was canceled. Such moves by local network affiliates reveal indifference to the Fairness Doctrine—a federal directive demanding broadcasters produce alternative points of view on social issues in order to maintain their licenses—when confronted with the competition of at least 200 different channels.

New Opportunities

With such shaky broadcasting prospects, what's the prognosis for Black-oriented media in the next century? We believe it depends on what partnerships African Americans decide to create. For instance, a partnership between historically Black Howard University and Kent State University, a majority white institution, helps keep *VillageAmerica,* a weekly public affairs show for people of color which premiered in 2002, on public television's national airwaves. Also, *BET Nightly News* is a partnership between Viacom properties BET and CBS.

Although Black-owned print media did not experience significant growth in the 1990s, some were able to create alternative media outlets on the World Wide Web. Black owned websites such as *The Black World Today* and *BlackPressUSA.com* continued to serve as Black daily "newspapers" on the World Wide Web. And while *Emerge: Black America's Newsmagazine,* folded in 2000, its editor, George E. Curry, moved on in 2001 to help revitalize the National Newspaper Publishers Association (NNPA) News Service, the wire service of 200 Black newspapers.

The survival of the Black press on and off the Internet seems especially critical in light of the void that exists in the print media. Except for *The Final Call,* the weekly organ of the Nation of Islam; *Jet,* an entertainment publication that has a news section; and *The Crisis,* the bimonthly organ of the national NAACP, there is still no national daily or weekly Black newspaper or national newsmagazine.

This combination—this convergence—of different print and web mediums should benefit African Americans because it provides additional forums for ideas, exchange, and debate. Instead of being held captive by BET or by cost-cutting managers at network affiliates, these developments suggest that African Americans are finding new and innovative ways to exert control over Black images.

1   Ken Gibbs, "Chuck D: Still Fighting the Power," *Africana.com*, March 28, 2001. http://www.africana.com/DailyArticles/index_20010328.htm.

2   Davey D, "BET Announces Sweeping Changes," bogus email sent via the Internet, April 1, 2002.

3   Sallie Hofmeister, "Viacom Expands Cable Empire with BET Purchase," *Los Angeles Times*, November 4, 2000, C1, Home edition.

4   Adam Zagorin, "BETs Too Hot A Property," *Time*, October 20, 1997, 80. In the year 2000, BET reached 58.5 million households. More than 70 percent of American homes now have basic cable television. In 2000, the *Los Angeles Times* quoted a study by an ad-buying firm that stated Black household subscriptions to cable exceeded white household subscriptions by 33 percent. See Greg Braxton, "Cable May Get Darts With Laurels Tonight," *Los Angeles Times*, April 14, 2000, F10.

5   Douglas Kellner, *Television and the Crisis of Democracy* (Boulder, CO: Westview Press, Inc., 1990).

6   *Not Just a Moral Imperative* (Reston, VA: Newspaper Association of America, 1994). NAA, The Newspaper Center, 11600 Sunrise Valley Drive, Reston, VA 22091-1412.

7   Children Now, *A Different World: Children's Perception of Race and Class in the Media* (Oakland, CA: Children Now, 1998).

8   Ben H. Bagdikian, *The Media Monopoly*, 5th ed. (Boston: Beacon Press, 1997).

9   Hal Hinson, "Amid a Long Drought, A Flowering of Talent," *New York Times*, February 17, 2002, sec. 2, p. 38.

10 Conversation with Kathy Nickens, adminstrative assistant to NABOB Executive Director James Winston, on May 31, 2002. Nickens said there were 220 Black-owned commercial stations and 20 television stations in the United States. She said, however, that all of them may not be active NABOB members in 2002.

11 One company, Clear Channel Communications, owns more than 1,200 of the nation's estimated 13,000 radio stations. Its syndication arm, Premiere Radio Network, syndicates politically conservative commentators Rush Limbaugh and Michael Reagan, one of the sons of former President Ronald Reagan.

12 Suzanne C. Ryan, "Channel 7 Reinstates 'Urban Update,'" *Boston Globe*, October 19, 2001, C2.

Chapter 11

Black Radicalism, Reinvented

The Promise of the Black Radical Congress

Jennifer Hamer and Clarence Lang

> We recognize the diverse historical tendencies in the Black radical tradition including revolutionary nationalism, feminism, and socialism.
>
> —Black Radical Congress, Principles of Unity, Point #1

Political scientist Robert C. Smith argues that three broad ideological traditions have shaped the Black Liberation Movement over time—liberal integrationism, nationalism, and radicalism. The strength and influence of each has ebbed and flowed in relation to Black America's social, political, and economic circumstances at a given historical period.

The political climate of the late 1970s and 1980s largely sidelined black radical politics, though many left organizations themselves aided and abetted this demise through dogmatism and other political errors. The degeneration, and eventual collapse, of the Soviet Union added to socialism's disrepute, while Western ideologues proclaimed the triumph of liberal bourgeois democracy and capitalism, and the essential "end of history." In 1997, however, a coalition of activist-scholars, labor, community organizers, and students attempted to regroup the scattered forces of the Black left and reassert its progressive political tradition. This project took bodily form in the Black Radical Congress (BRC).[1]

The coalition's birth, and its growing pains, have provided observers and participants with important subject matter for both popular and scholarly articles, for at this historical moment the Congress remains one of the most ambitious Black radical formations.[2] The effort to build such a united front was itself a response to American globalist political-economic policies abroad, the depressingly rightward drift in US politics during the Reagan-Bush-Clinton years, and the attendant decline in African Americans' conditions of life. The BRC has also represented a bold attempt to articulate a theoretical and strategic alternative to the liberal rapprochement of the National Association for the Advancement of Colored People (NAACP) and the militant Black conservativism of the Nation of Islam (NOI). The Congress' presence marks a potential shift in a constant, yet currently faint, movement. Despite its early promise and considerable successes at the opening of a new millennium, this united front faces a number of formidable challenges. This essay discusses the circumstances of the BRC's development, its strengths, weaknesses, current state, and continuing relevance to progressive politics.[3]

The Historical Period

> The technological revolution and capitalist globalization have changed the economy, labor force, and class formations that need to inform our analysis and strategies. The increased class polarization created by these developments demand that we, as Black radicals, ally ourselves with the most oppressed sectors of our communities and society.
> —Black Radical Congress, Principles of Unity, Point #2

The Black Radical Congress' entry onto the stage of history was timely, particularly given the corrosive elements striking Black communities in the 1980s, the '90s, and into the new century. This period, characterized by the consolidation of an American globalist order, has witnessed a growing backlash to the political and economic gains that people of color, women, and labor made primarily as a result of mass movements during the middle decades of the twentieth century. Since then, Black people and families have experienced growing isolation and the loss of civil and social rights in varying forms. Between 1980 and 1993, federal spending on employment and training programs was cut nearly in half, while spending on corrections increased by 521 percent. By the mid-1990s, Marc Mauer writes, "half of the inmates in the nation's prisons were African American, compared to their 13 percent share of the population, and one in fourteen adult black males was locked up in prison or jail on any given day." From 1985 to 1995, he notes a 143 percent increase in the number of Black men in federal and state prisons. A staggering 204 percent increase occurred in the number of Black women behind bars, where they have faced sexual violence at the hands of their keepers.[4]

Corporate downsizing, industrial layoffs, and urban fiscal crisis forced many Black men and women into unemployment lines, temporary employment agencies, and low-paying, casual labor markets. During the early 1990s the unemployment rate for Black men and women was twice that of their white counterparts (Employers report a preference for hiring Asians and Hispanics over African Americans, mainly based on continuing stereotypes about Black labor.)[5] Means-tested social programs and racist constructions of the "welfare queen" have stigmatized Black working-class mothers.[6] These decaying social conditions have thrust more of them into illegal economies, where they have been victims of violence, even murder, at the hands of men.

Between 1999 and 2001, twelve women were murdered in the St. Louis-East St. Louis metropolitan area, their bodies dumped in abandoned houses, empty fields, and beneath train trestles. Each of the victims, save one, was Black. Most allegedly sold sex when they needed money. At this writing, the murders remain unsolved. Young Black girls have not escaped sexual crime either. In nearby Bethalto, a thirteen-year-old was assaulted—not once, but twice—by three white males, the oldest in his twenties. The blithe attitude of local police and the district attorney's office led a predominantly white grand jury to not indict the men, citing lack of physical evidence. The issues involved in this case awakened historical memories of the rape of Black women, and the apathy of the justice system.[7]

Diminished life chances greet those newly born as well. In 1975, the infant mortality rate for African Americans was almost twice that of whites. By the early 1990s, it had increased to almost two and half times the rate of whites. At the dawn of the new millennium, approximately one-third of Black children in the United States lived in poverty. For many of those who survived infancy, academic potential suffered due to lead poisoning and asthma, both of which affect Black communities disproportionately. Black youth were also 1.3 times as likely as whites to drop out of high school—one of the many consequences of underfunded public schools and declining community resources for cultural and social development. Alternative schools for students with special needs, the foster care system, and group homes are filled with Black youth. These factors have lent themselves to maintaining a lucrative and deadly drug trade in many urban communities—at levels of both supply and demand.[8]

Meanwhile, more Black grandmothers were taking responsibility for children as their daughters succumbed to HIV infection and AIDS at a rate outstripping all other women. Black fathers were more likely to see their sons go to juvenile correctional facilities and prisons than to college. Life was not getting better with the advance of age either. Compared to their white counterparts, elderly African Americans were more likely to suffer heart disease, debilitating strokes, diabetes complications, and related ailments. They were also more likely to die in poverty. Exacerbating these conditions, the federal government under the Bill Clinton administration instituted the Personal Responsibility and Work Opportunity Reconciliation Act of 1996. This act began the systematic removal of low-income parents and their children from public assistance, casting them into the uncertain world of "workfare" where private sector wages often prove insufficient for basic needs.[9]

The privatization of entitlements for the poor and working class has occurred alongside Black people's marginalization from public space and accommodations. Developers and residents of predominantly white communities have privatized common space through numerous means, including "gated" public roads that prevent Black and Brown people from entering, or even passing through, their cities and neighborhoods.[10] In Chicago, Detroit, New York, St. Louis, and other major cities, pro-growth coalitions are destroying affordable public housing to make way for corporate offices, university and hospital expansions, stadiums, and private dwellings for upper-income professionals. Many Black urban families, who comprise an exceedingly large share of low-income residents, have borne the brunt of this inner-city displacement.

These conditions are symbolic of the same patterns of exclusion behind the dismantling of public recreation sites on the fringes of affluent communities; racial profiling by police and private security officers; police harassment of youth at all-Black gatherings; "gang" antiloitering laws; and the outright dilution of the Black vote during the 2000 elections upheld by the US Supreme Court. Even many among the Black professional-managerial class have faced exclusion, though perhaps differently. More than any other group they exist one paycheck away from poverty regardless of education and income. Overall, African Americans find themselves being pushed further and further to the social, political, and economic margins of society. Certainly, the practices and policies described above do not constitute an outright return to Jim Crow, the particular system of racial control that thrived between the 1890s and 1960s. Nonetheless, African Americans have encountered a new form of segregation within the body politic, contributing to declining quality-of-life conditions.[11]

At the end of the twentieth century, Black people were struggling, as in the past, to maintain and improve basic civil and social rights—to health care, shelter, the vote, education, better wages, and job security. While the social and economic ills of most Black communities reached epidemic proportions, the Black left was painfully absent in national discourse. Black leadership was dominated by those who either sought accommodation with the right, or echoed the dominant Republican themes of "personal responsibility" and "self-help," as in the case of the Million Man March. The Black Radical Congress took shape against this backdrop.[12]

A "Center Without Walls": The Call to Rebuild a Movement

> If you believe in the politics of Black liberation, join us in Chicago in 1998 at the Black Radical Congress. If you hate what capitalism has done to our community—widespread joblessness, drugs, violence and poverty—come to the Congress. If you are fed up with the corruption of the two party system and want to develop a plan for real political change, come to the Congress. If you want to struggle against class exploitation, racism, sexism, and homophobia, come to the Congress. The Black Radical Congress is for everyone ready to fight back: trade unionists and workers, youth and students, women, welfare recipients, lesbians and gays, public housing tenants and the homeless, the elderly and people on fixed incomes, veterans, cultural workers, and immigrants. You!
>
> —Black Radical Congress, *The Struggle Continues: Setting a Black Liberation Agenda for the 21st Century,* leaflet, circa 1997-1998.

Responding to this call, workers, activists, students, youth, and intellectuals around the nation assembled local organizing committees in anticipation of the BRC's inaugural meeting. During Juneteenth weekend 1998, 2,000 of them gathered in Chicago with the goal of developing and adopting a Black radical agenda for the 21st Century. Members of the coalition affirmed collective "Principles of Unity," and a rough-draft "Black Freedom Agenda" reflecting a general vision of radical social transformation. In the period since its public debut, this united front has offered profound critiques of global capitalism, US politics, persistent patriarchy, the marginalization of Black America, and current international crises.

Most significantly, BRC activists developed a vast and lively cyberspace community.[13] As with any entity in motion, the internet has brought with it the danger of exclusion (or worse yet, chaos and confusion), but also the potential for mass participation. The BRC's numerous email list-serves have facilitated not only wide-ranging debate on the pressing issues of the day, but also the distribution of press releases and critical analyses to thousands of people. The coalition's national newsletter, *BRC Today,* provided an additional forum in which members shared experiences, analyses, and lessons learned through local activities. Activists used similar outlets to discuss sexual violence against Black women, the case for reparations for slavery and continuing social violence against African Americans, and the revolutionary potential of hip hop culture and the internet. More generally, the Congress' presence animated new theoretical explorations of Black radicalism itself, and gave renewed legitimacy to the scholar-activist tradition in Black Studies.[14]

In the few years since its formation, the BRC has built a sterling reputation for insightful radical political analysis and courageous political positions—on the continuing Israeli-Palestinian conflict, Black voting patterns in a period of growing Latino electoral power, the legal coup that installed George W. Bush in the White House, and the implications of the United States' present war against Afghanistan. A very loose network of local BRC committees, caucuses, and affiliated organizations has matched its theoretical work with concrete organizing efforts on the ground: Chicago, St. Louis, New York, Detroit, Sacramento, Los Angeles, Knoxville, Atlanta, Louisville, and Oakland are among the cities that have boasted a BRC presence. These various bodies have tackled pressing local and national concerns, including police brutality, reparations, and the displacement of Black tenants and families for urban "revitalization" projects.[15]

Others launched a short-lived book project, *The State of Afro-America: Radical Perspectives,* geared toward diffusing the views of a broad Black left, and raising revenue for the coalition (A BRC speakers bureau was another proposed fundraiser.)[16] For a while, one well-placed member used his press connections to facilitate the airing of Black radical perspectives on various newspaper editorial pages.

Small groupings of BRC activists rallied strongly around a union struggle in Charleston, South Carolina that merged issues of Black civil rights, the political repression of activists, and the dignity of organized labor.[17] BRC activists in Detroit were involved in a 10,000-strong protest at a local mall following the murder of a Black man by security guards. In another action, they helped turn out an overflow crowd at a City Council discussion on living wages.[18] Elsewhere in the region, the Congress' Toledo chapter has been at the forefront of a "cyber-organizing" strategy built on establishing Black community technology centers.[19] Members of the BRC's Black Feminist Caucus mobilized support behind Tabitha Walrond, a young Black mother arrested in the starvation death of her infant. As feminists argued, the real culprits were urban inequality and welfare policies regarding health care.[20] BRC members in Philadelphia have participated in coalition work to stop the planned execution of political prisoner Mumia Abu-Jamal.

In a similar vein, the "Hands Off Assata!" campaign coordinated by Chicago-area BRC activists, has fought efforts by US officials to extradite a former Black Panther from political refuge in Cuba. By tying Assata Shakur's case to the FBI's Counterintelligence Program that illegally harassed and imprisoned activists, the campaign highlights the continuing legacies of state-sponsored repression in the United States. In the long term, many activists hoped the BRC's many initiatives could expand and deepen the its base among the broadest community of black people, and set an example for other progressive forces.[21]

Following the BRC's National Organizing Conference in Detroit during the early summer of 2000, local organizing committees assumed responsibility for advancing the BRC's newly adopted national campaign, "Education, Not Incarceration: Fight the Police State!" The result of two difficult years of debate and planning, the campaign sought to challenge the overlapping trends of privatization, state-sponsored violence, and the loss of civil and social rights. It consisted of five components. The first was a petition to make police brutality and misconduct a federal crime, with a goal of at least 100,000 signatures. The second component involved a commitment to support defense work on behalf of the "Charleston Five," Black longshoremen charged with felonies for their part in a planned picket against a union-busting shipping firm. The criminal charges they faced stemmed from a police-instigated confrontation with workers. The third aspect of the national campaign revolved around a boycott of the multinational Sodexho Mariott Services, which at the time was a major corporate investor in private, for-profit prisons in the United States. Fourth, the campaign called for organized opposition to publicly funded private education, in the form of vouchers and similar methods of corporate control. Finally, the campaign focused on generating attention to the ways in which Black women fall prey to legal and extra-legal violence. The diverse elements of this national campaign were not at all incongruous. Common to all of these campaign elements was the recognition that police violence, repression, and incarceration, form a linchpin to racial exclusion, gender oppression, and working people's declining economic conditions.[22]

The BRC's potential to lead the Black Liberation Movement into the 21st century was indeed tremendous, and it still carries the potential to move the Black radical tradition in exciting new directions. Since its founding, the BRC has made the ending of women's oppression one of its central tenets of struggle. Its Principles of Unity, Freedom Agenda, and similar documents firmly acknowledge gender, race, class, and sexual orientation as interlocking systems of oppression and exploitation. As a statement of policy, BRC leadership has committed itself to an antisexist and antiheterosexist program, though with some exceptions gendered divisions of labor have persisted alongside certain masculinist political styles. The Congress' foremost strength was the diversity of its rank-and-file, a vibrant mixture of revolutionary nationalists, feminists, left-leaning liberals, and various socialists. A number of leading members hailed from cadre and mass-based organizations, or university and journalist networks—Freedom Road Socialist Organization, New Afrikan People's Organization, Organization for Black Struggle, Ida B. Wells-W.E.B. DuBois Network, Malcolm X Grassroots Movement, *News & Letters,* League of Revolutionaries for a New America, Committees of Correspondence, Communist Party USA, *Labor Notes,* Project South, and Black Workers for Justice. Many others, however, were independent "free radicals" without formal organizational ties.

Beyond its heterogeneity, the BRC was endowed at birth with immense resources. Leadership and rank-and-file membership brought high levels of formal education, prestige, celebrity, skills, and institutional support. Veteran activists, presumably, brought to the coalition years of practical experience that could be placed at the disposal of newer activists. Early in its development, the BRC's general membership also crossed generational boundaries. At the

1998 Congress, hundreds of youth filled the corridors of the University of Illinois-Chicago campus, visited workshops and sessions, and exchanged thoughts and experiences with those much older than themselves. However tenuously, the BRC's Principles of Unity managed to consolidate a number of diverse trends into a "center without walls," hewn around a common vision of social change and transformation. The coalition's Freedom Agenda, though an incomplete document, nonetheless reflected a comprehensive program of action.

Wanted: A Radical Strategic Vision

> Black radicals must build a national congress of radical forces in the Black community to strengthen radicalism as the legitimate voice of Black working and poor people, and to build organized resistance.
> —Black Radical Congress, Principles of Unity, Point #11

Despite its resources, emancipatory vision, and agenda, the BRC sorely lacked a coordinated strategy for implementing any practical program. The "Education, Not Incarceration!" campaign actually reflected a compromise among those who demanded a focus on police brutality, others who called for an emphasis on education, and a core of feminists who wanted to highlight the issue of violence against African American women by the state and by black men. These themes were all obviously related; yet, the interconnections among them were articulated after the fact, rather than plotted systematically. As other elements were successively added, the campaign devolved into a hodgepodge of countervailing activities—too much for one fledgling coalition to reasonably undertake. This compounded the failure by BRC national leadership to execute a coherent plan of action, though the coalition's National Campaign Committee articulated one.

Following the September 11, 2001 attacks on the World Trade Center and Pentagon, and the US war launched against Afghanistan in early October, the contours of the campaign were altered. Rather than using the moment to highlight the danger of an expanded domestic police state under the banner of "fighting terrorism," BRC leadership deemphasized the petition against police violence and misconduct. The new emphasis became an unspecified opposition to "war and terror." A few—including one BRC chapter in New York, and a BRC-affiliated organization in St. Louis—continued to mobilize around the "Education Not Incarceration" through conferences or local efforts for police control boards.

But in the absence of a coordinated national campaign, these initiatives have been disparate. Whatever the intentions, the confusion involved in reshuffling campaign emphases has contributed to demoralizing previously active members. It also has affected the coalition's ability to systematically recruit and retain new members. This, unfortunately, is not a new problem. By the end of its third year, the BRC had 15 local organizing committees, but only a handful functioned. Participation by the majority of original Congress-goers proved short-lived. In less than a year, membership rolls dropped precipitously.

Although the BRC's initial call successfully emphasized building local organizing committees and nurturing a mass base, subsequent BRC activities did little to sustain this effect. Beyond a handful of motivated individuals, national leadership often failed to lead, or rather guide, collective discussion toward attainable political objectives. Other coalition members compounded the problem by not taking up the tasks necessary to move work forward. This factor, along with a lack of support among most leadership, was responsible for the demise of the national newsletter. Local organizing committees were charged with fundraising, recruitment, and local publicity.

However, few resources for skills building and training were allocated to support them in these tasks. The actual training of activists has taken center stage only once in the BRC's short history—at its National Organizing Conference in Detroit, and then only during a one-day workshop. As of this writing, the BRC still lacks a formal program of political education for its members. Organizational practice suffered, further, from a lack of clear and consistent communication among the BRC's national leadership bodies, caucuses, and local organizing committees.[23] This issue has yet to be resolved. Likewise, ascertaining what tasks most of the BRC's national leaders actually do, and their effectiveness, proved difficult, if not impossible. In this atmosphere, general membership grew increasingly isolated from, and mistrustful of, national leadership. Members' numerous other obligations also affected their ability to sustain local committees. Men and women joined the BRC as full-time workers, parents, students, spouses, and activists in other organizations. Balancing BRC work with these other responsibilities often proved overwhelming, and many members have struggled with integrating BRC work with other aspects of their political lives. The hardest task some BRC activists have faced has been convincing potential recruits (and fellow members!) that the Congress exists as a united front to enhance the political work they are already doing, and not an attempt to supplant it.

A mass-based coalition must necessarily plant its roots among the broadest numbers of people living in our communities, most of whom are working class and poor.[24] Though perhaps involved in the BRC at a grassroots level, they have been largely underrepresented in its governing bodies, and at national meetings where members make important decisions about policy and direction. Local organizing committee representatives have been required to travel great distances to attend these meetings. Even those who can marshal resources to travel—university professors and labor union officials, for instance—have done so often at a financial loss. Those who have less income and institutional support at their disposal—paralegals, low-level social workers, and elementary school teachers—have attended these national meetings at an even greater loss. They frequently overextended personal budgets for travel and childcare, used valuable "sick" and "vacation" days from work, stretched credit cards to pay for lodging and meals, and spent long hours in transit.

The practice of scheduling the most critical agenda items on the last day of national meetings, when most people are heading home (due to work schedules or travel arrangements beyond their control) has also hindered broader participation in the past. This is all to say nothing of the municipal employees, home health workers, fast food cooks, hotel maids and doormen, and the unemployed, whose economic circumstances almost entirely bar them from involvement in the BRC at the national level. Needless to say, the voices of those who bear the brunt of the present socioeconomic and political crises were rarely part of discussions about organizational strategy, program, and internal practices. A disproportionate number of the BRC national leaders, even those with working-class roots, are part of the Black petty managerial and professional strata. Because of our socioeconomic status and relative prestige, and the lack of support for more inclusive decision-making, some of us have assumed the authority to speak for those capable of speaking for themselves.

Antiparticipatory impulses are in some ways an unavoidable phase in a political organization's development, where the ability to respond rapidly to changing conditions is vital. But in the absence of formal, serious reflection and self-criticism, such tendencies can become routine conduct, further undermining an organization's ability to sustain and expand its base. In the BRC's case, decisions have too often come from the top down, rather than from the bottom up.[25]

With few exceptions, the BRC's remaining local organizing committees are held together by small groupings of dedicated individuals struggling to build the coalition's mass character, but the lack of a functioning national infrastructure and strategic vision has taken a frustrating toll. There is little coordinated activity by the local committees, or even among them. This is in part a result of the weak and disorganized nature of many Black liberation and left organizations, both locally and nationally. Objectively, BRC activists came together because of these collective weaknesses, but subjectively most have never assessed the degree or types of weaknesses we share, or our strengths. In practice, consequently, the BRC has largely reacted to pressing crises, rather than advanced a consistent agenda of its own.[26]

The flood of events in a historical period can be overwhelming, and the current moment in the new millennium has been tumultuous enough to leave even veteran political activists reeling. Poll managers, police, the judicial system, and national and state officials were all complicit in violating Black voting rights in November

2000. In February 2001, David Horowitz and other right-wing commentators mounted a public offensive against the African American reparations campaign. For several days that spring, Black Cincinnati rebelled following the police shooting death of young Timothy Thomas.[27] That summer, the US State Department was visibly absent from the 2001 UN World Conference Against Racism in Durban, South Africa. "Nine-eleven" occurred several months later, giving impetus to a US militarism of the most cartoonish, action-figure variety—deadlier because no other global superpowers exist to keep it in check. In a likely effort to protect its generals and civilian leaders from possible war crimes charges related to the handling of Afghan and other future captives, the US State Department withdrew from the International Criminal Court in May 2002.[28]

Domestically, the war generated the development of a surreal, fascist-sounding "Homeland Security" office in the federal government. US intervention in the Mideast has also occasioned renewed attacks on domestic civil liberties, as witnessed in a new wave of repressive legislative measures like the USA PATRIOT Act of 2001, and the Enhanced Border Security and Visa Entry Reform Act of 2002.[29] The open-ended nature of the current presidential administration's "war on terrorism" augurs ill not only for immigrants and the charities and organizations that support them, but also for any foreign- or domestic-born individual or group identified as a "potential" threat.

A range of executive measures, meanwhile, has begun the erosion of even the pretense of due process and transparency in government decision-making. The Oval Office has supported the refusal, by Homeland Security chief Tom Ridge, to come before Congress. If enforced, one executive order would even limit access to presidential papers.[30] Concurrent scandals involving Enron and Arthur Andersen accounting have become emblematic of a number of catastrophic trends—visible corporate influence on the White House, public officials' open scorn of accountability to citizens, rising unemployment and shaky private retirement plans, and the skyrocketing costs of energy and fuel for working-class consumers.[31]

These international and domestic developments have all provided the Black Radical Congress opportunities to intervene in national discourse about race, structural inequalities, foreign policy, and power. However, the line between responding to events and being buffeted by social and political currents is a fine one. In the absence of any immediate wave to ride, the BRC has too often drifted. The hasty shift in its national campaign once again suggested the coalition lacked a strategic center.

Clearly, it would be short-sighted to dismiss the importance of the BRC's vocal opposition to the war, especially when liberal and conservative trends within the Black Liberation Movement have endorsed the US globalist war and foreign policy in Israel. Laws like the USA PATRIOT Act, and US support for Israeli aggression in the Occupied Territories, overlap with police terror in communities of color in the United States and the prison-industrial complex housing scores of Black and Brown people. The racist underpinnings of the war on terrorism directly mirrors those that have buttressed an equally vicious "war on drugs" responsible for rapid rates of incarceration among African Americans and Latinos. Both have siphoned resources away from spending on the public welfare, and threaten to bring an American police state into full-fledged being. Thus, the fight for social justice at home is indivisible from working toward alternatives to the US globalist policies that nurtured the rise of right-wing Islamic governments and networks abroad and buttressed the state terrorism of US foreign allies.[32]

But all political groupings, and certainly radical organizations, have to reconcile the need to respond to ever-changing conditions against the necessity of charting a consistent course. The alternative is a flurry of good activity, but no force of momentum. Successfully organizing a base has to proceed directly from the experiences and concerns salient to the broadest numbers within a targeted group. In confronting state-sponsored terrorism against Black communities, the BRC's national petition for a federal law against police crimes and misconduct had this essential characteristic. Few of us were naïve enough to believe it would result in any immediate policy changes, or that a federal law would alone solve the problem of police violence. The much larger aim was building broad constituencies, as opposed to simply claiming them. Even in the worst case scenario, circulating the petition contained the potential of routinizing contact with those critical to our long-term success: the everyday people who are not already yet politically engaged, but may be willing to fight for proposals that speak directly to their material existence. Black parents want to protect their children from pollutants, poor nutrition, ill health, and underfunded schools. Black adults want to earn decent pay and employment benefits. Many retirement age Black men and women worry about the inability to meet the high costs of heating, air conditioning, and medical expenses. Such "home sphere" issues have historically been the root of mass protests in Black communities.

The point is that overlapping initiatives against US global hegemony, including antiwar support, could have radiated from a programmatic center around the petition or some similar concrete initiative. Without a cogent plan of action, activists forfeit the ability to carry out an independent agenda, one that can command attention in our communities and strengthen our position in national and international affairs. Without this grounding, we easily end up issuing politically sophisticated, though essentially toothless, demands for those in power to act more democratically.

Internal Political Culture

> We must be democratic and inclusive in our dealings with one another, making room for constructive criticism and honest dissent within our ranks. There must be open venues for civil and comradely debates to occur.
> —Black Radical Congress, Principles of Unity, Point #7

The BRC's weaknesses have stemmed from more than its infrastructural and strategic problems. As a coalition, we may have ruthlessly shone the spotlight on the contradictions of global capitalism. Yet, as indicated above, we have not demonstrated an ability to interrogate our own internal political practices with similar precision and depth. BRC activists have made demands of US political and economic institutions that many of us have apparently been unwilling to implement within our own ranks. Proportional representation, participatory democracy, and new gender relations provide several examples.

On the whole, the BRC has set a standard for openness. Nevertheless, within the BRC's first year, many active members voiced a growing uneasiness with a trend toward centralization of procedure and decision-making within the coalition's leadership bodies. As discussed above, this impulse may reflect a historical trend within Black united fronts. Even still, it has not proved an effective means of maintaining any alliance of socialists, nationalists, and others who participate with expectations of full inclusion. To take an example: While the decision to meet quarterly for national decision-making may initially have been most practical, many representatives have clearly been unable to commit to such travel.

And in the past, the scheduling of key agenda items on the last day of meetings has contributed to the appearance of political exclusion—a perception fostered by a disconnect already existing among various levels of BRC leadership and the rank-and-file. No one would expect Black radicals to remain passive if the local city council or NAACP engaged in activities that marginalized members of the community in impact, if not intent—as in scheduling meetings on sensitive matters in the middle of a work day. Certainly, no one should expect Black radicals to say nothing when similar activities occur within their own political household. The BRC's national meeting and agenda arrangements, then, have been an obstacle to internal cohesion. More important still, they have been contradictory to building a mass-based coalition, especially if recruiting working-class and low-income members remains a goal.[33]

In the assessment of some national BRC leaders, fundraising should be among the coalition's top priorities to address activists' limited means of travel, with local organizing committees assuming primary responsibility. But these bodies have struggled for cohesion themselves. In the past, at least, the small number of participants in many local committees have not only restricted the areas of work members can assume, but also accentuated old and new ideological-political grudges and personal differences. The failure to recruit new and younger members typically allowed such problems to fester and explode. Thus, several locals have split into separate BRC entities, or fizzled altogether. This has been but a local manifestation of a much larger problem of managing diversity within a national coalition.[34]

From the outset, undercurrents of favoritism existed at the national level, particularly toward an overlapping left-wing liberal/social democratic tendency and certain university-based networks. Individuals within this clique in the past trivialized legitimate questions about strategy, and differing theoretical perspectives, as troublemaking or asserting "special" interests. Others engaged in petty personal attacks on perceived political opponents. Leadership since the founding Congress had either actively or passively assented to this behavior, in part out of an understandable fear of splitting the coalition. With increasing frequency, however, members from other political trends publicly demanded the coalition ensure that democratic procedures were practiced in all BRC bodies, and by all ideological-political tendencies—whether they were majorities, minorities, or "unknowns."[35]

In a related vein, personality politics emerged as an intractable problem. To a certain extent, they have always been present within the BRC, and for the most part subtle. Yet, it was disturbing to see a few academic intellectuals engage in practices diametrically opposed to the subject matter they teach, and the scholarship they write, all in the name of defending someone "respectable" against criticism. "Sectarianism"—a genuine problem in previous left organizations and Black united front efforts—became an all-purpose shibboleth for denigrating questions about practices and policies raised by individuals outside of a few national organizations and affinity groups.[36]

Bruising conflicts about representation and participation emerged earliest within two BRC caucuses—Youth and Feminist. The political and regional schisms among youth participants in the BRC were evident at the founding Congress in 1998, and arguably were more disruptive than anything else that occurred that weekend in Chicago. Open factionalism continued after the Juneteenth meeting. A functioning Youth Caucus became the ultimate casualty in a political "cyber-war" that continued through the summer, gradually petering out by the fall.

Many aspects of this internal "line struggle" were in fact healthy. The debates, for instance, yielded a concrete proposal for an Organizers' Institute, which became a basis for the day-long workshop held at the BRC's 2000 Organizing Conference in Detroit. The problem with the conflict, however, lay in the fact that no formal mechanisms existed for resolving internal differences. Thus, when political lines were drawn in the sand, the majority of youth—who had few preexisting political or ideological commitments—quietly opted to withdraw, depriving the BRC of its most vital demographic component. In the summer of 2000, a core of organized youth reconstituted the caucus. Even still, with the possible exception of one area of the south, Youth Caucus activity remains scattered. Many Black youth are indeed politically engaged. Unfortunately, that engagement has occurred largely outside the auspices of the BRC.

A similar course of events occurred within the Black Feminist Caucus (BFC). From its inception, the BFC advocated an antisexist and antipatriarchal society, and demanded the same within the united front. However, a number of caucus members failed to institute these elements within their own ranks. The result was often a "patriarchal" form of feminism. While arguing for the multiplicity of identities, caucus practices suggested that many members valued only one feminism. As with the Youth Caucus, no formal mechanisms existed here for resolving disputes, and within the first year the BFC fell into quietude, despite the continuing use of internet list-serves and occasional meetings. In retrospect, the implosion of both the Youth and Feminist caucuses foreshadowed the crisis that has afflicted the BRC more generally.

Part of the problem of internal political culture flows from the fact that BRC activists have not acknowledged explicitly enough the complexity of the Congress-building process. The BRC is not an organization as such, where one would expect more ideological coherence. Rather, it is a broad alliance of diverse left tendencies. In this kind of situation, the balance of power is always shifting as these tendencies recede or surge in strength, or form sub-alliances.

The problem develops when the dominant faction of the moment ceases efforts to reach a genuine rapprochement with other tendencies. The failure to squarely address this contradiction, in addition to the lack of an overall strategic vision, became painfully clear in the summer of 2001, when a heated debate erupted about the prospect of receiving a grant from a major private foundation.

Views among the national leadership ran the gamut. Some endorsed accepting the grant on the grounds of pragmatic necessity; besides, they reasoned, the movement had a right to some of the corporate elite wealth created by Black labor. Others expressed a steadfast opposition to taking funds from a major foundation, based on previous experiences with cooptive corporate liberalism.[37] A number of participants in the debate reflected gradations between these two poles. Embedded in the dispute also was the question of what type of organization-building the BRC would adopt—a "corporate" model serving to distance the coalition from a real constituency, or a "movement" model premised on mass organization. The situation became exceptionally charged because a few, who supported accepting the funding, attempted an earlier end run around collective deliberations. Their suggestion was that concerns about falling into a quicksand of soft money, or misgivings about the procedural issues involved in the discussion, were simply "sectarian," or worse yet, "infantile." While the debate ended without definite resolution, the preexisting weaknesses that brought this matter to a boil persist.

Conclusion: Reinventing the Black Radical Congress

> To be "radical" means to get at the root of real problems, seeking effective solutions.
>
> —Black Radical Congress, *Black Freedom Agenda*
> *for the Twenty First Century,* Draft, 1998.

Our inability to honestly address the coalition's many faults—a troubled strategic vision, a national leadership ineffective at coordinating communication and activity among BRC bodies, and an unhealthy internal culture—was responsible for the BRC's stagnancy and loss of focus after the dispute about foundation funding.

In the absence of a comprehensive base-building strategy, a discussion about a potential grant easily dominated cyberspace discussion, longer than any group with a clear direction and constituency might have allowed. The failure of national leadership to serve its purpose enabled mere individuals to substitute for the will of the BRC's chief governing body, and structure the terms of discussion. An unhealthy internal political culture made us vulnerable to a debilitating debate characterized by false analogies, denials, shallow personality politics, and mutual distrust. These problems, lingering since 1998, have led to a gradual corrosion of the BRC's political diversity and base.

Yet the BRC can overcome these fetters on its development with sober and forthright assessments about the state of our movement. Processing where we have been can strengthen the resolve and motivation of activists, for political movements are not only about social transformation, but also the self-transformation of movement activists themselves. Much of the BRC's hope lay in reinforcing our Principles of Unity and Freedom Agenda. Strategically, this current moment in history demands a Black radical strategy that commits local and national energies to a clearly defined and concrete goal, one that serves multiple purposes: the raising of political awareness, particularly among those who have little or no political engagement; recruitment, especially of newer and younger activists; and the courting of support among the broadest numbers of people across lines of race and nationality. Second, we stand in need of a program of practical skills building for the arduous period ahead, one that draws on, as well as advances, the skills of both newer and older activists. Comprehensive study of national and local political economies, African American history, and the history of the Black Liberation Movement should all become subjects in a long-term program of study.

We need a new paradigm of politics based on a genuine feminism. All participants, whether in leadership or the rank-and-file, have valuable roles to play in the BRC. Their ability to fulfill them relies on the kind of structures we build. Hierarchical structures often silence participants, and contribute to a Great Man (or even Great Woman) view of history and social movements. This type of personality politics should have no role in a radical organization; it is both antiparticipatory and antifeminist. Finally, if it is "unity" that self-described radicals truly desire among themselves, members of the BRC coalition should struggle both openly and collectively for it. Rigidity, silence, or seeking to represent one political line as the "common sense" will not produce it. If anything, these responses derail solidarity and political growth. Unity is something only achieved through renewing the BRC's political diversity and implementing radical democratic procedures. The central choice this historical moment presents Black radical activists is whether to respond to the initiatives of the state, or blaze our own strategic path; concede to becoming a loose email discussion group, or fight to construct a radical model of organization derived from our movement.

The authors give special thanks to Sundiata Keita Cha-Jua, Helen Neville, and Connie White. Many of the arguments made in this article are the culmination of collective discussions, theoretical papers, or joint BRC work with these and other comrades. Special thanks also to Robert Chrisman for his insights into a number of issues discussed here.

1 Robert C. Smith, "Ideology as the Enduring Dilemma of Black Politics," in George A. Persons (ed.), *Dilemmas of Black Politics: Issues of Leadership and Strategy* (New York: HarperCollins, 1993), 211-224; Alex Callinicos, *Theories and Narratives: Reflections on the Philosophy of History* (Durham: Duke University Press, 1995); and Francis Fukuyama, *The End of History and the Last Man* (New York: Avon, 1992).

2 Manning Marable, "The Black Radical Congress: Revitalizing the Black Freedom Movement," *The Black Scholar*, Vol. 28, No. 1 (Spring 1998): 54-70; Angela Ards, "The New Black Radicalism," *The Nation*, July 27-August 3, 1998, 19-23; Salim Muwakkil, "Where Do We Go from Here? Developing a Left Politics for African-Americans," *In These Times*, July 12, 1998, 14-16; and Michael Eric Dyson, "Pulpit Politics: Religion and the Black Radical Tradition," *In These Times*, July 12, 1998, 17-19; David Bacon, "The Progressive Interview: Bill Fletcher," *The Progressive*, March 2000, 31-35. See also *The Black Scholar's* special issue on the BRC, Vol. 28, No. 3-4 (Fall-Winter 1998).

3 See Sundiata Keita Cha-Jua and Clarence Lang, "Providence, Patriarchy, Pathology: Louis Farrakhan's Rise & Decline," *New Politics*, Vol. 6, No. 2 (Winter 1997): 47-71; Sundiata Keita Cha-Jua, "The Black Radical Congress and the Reconstruction of the Black Freedom Movement, *The Black Scholar*, Vol. 28, No. 3-4 (Fall-Winter 1998): 8-21; Sundiata Keita Cha-Jua and Clarence Lang, "Strategies for Black Liberation in the Era of Globalism: Retronouveau Civil Rights, Militant Black Conservatism, and Radicalism," *The Black Scholar*, Vol. 29, No. 4 (Winter 1999): 25-47; and Clarence Lang, "The New Global and Urban Order: Legacies for the 'Hip-Hop Generation'," *Race & Society*, Vol. 3 (2000): 111-142. Globalism, a new phase of capitalist accumulation ascendant since the mid-1970s, is characterized by the cutting of state spending for social welfare, the parceling of state-owned enterprises to the private sector, and the breaking down of trade barriers, especially those limiting advanced economies' access to developing peripheries. In a globalist economy, multilateral institutions like the International Monetary Fund and World Bank permeate nation-state boundaries, and service-based production supplants manufacturing.

4 Marc Maurer, *Race to Incarcerate* (New York: The New Press, 1999), 68, 124-125. See also Helen A. Neville and Jennifer Hamer, 'We Make Freedom': An Exploration of Revolutionary Black Feminism," *Journal of Black Studies*, Vol. 31, No. 4 (March 2001): 437-461

5 Philip Moss and Chris Tilly, *Stories Employers Tell: Race, Skill, and Hiring in America* (New York: Russell Sage Foundation, 2001); Harry J. Holzer, *What Employers Want: Job Prospects for Less-Educated Workers* (New York: Russell Sage Foundation, 1996); and Marc Bendick, Charles W. Jackson, and Victor A. Reinoso, "Measuring Employment Discrimination Through Controlled Experiments," *Review of Black Political Economy*, Vol. 23 (Summer 1994): 25-48.

6 Karen Seccombe, Delores James, and Kimberly Battle Walters, 'They Think You Ain't Much of Nothing': The Social Construction of the Welfare Mother," *Journal of Marriage and the Family* 60 (November 1998): 849-865.

7 Susan Skiles Luke, "East St. Louis Police Struggle to Solve Deaths of 12 Women," Associated Press, January 6, 2002; Bill Smith, "Slain Woman's Life Played Out Along Broadway in Baden," *St. Louis Post-Dispatch,* May 19, 2002, C1-C4; Jennifer Hamer, "Rape and Race in the 21st Century," *The Black World Today,* www.tbwt.com, reprinted in *The Final Call,* June 26, 2001, 23.

8 See Dorothy Roberts, *Shattered Bonds: The Color of Child Welfare* (New York: Basic Books, 2002). For a thorough review of health among Black Americans see Ronald L. Braithwaite and Sandra Taylor (eds.), *Health Issues in the Black Community,* second edition (San Francisco: Jossey-Bass Publishers, 2001).

9 See *The State of Black America* (National Urban League, 1998); Cedric Herring, "African Americans in Contemporary America: Progress and Retrenchment," in Anthony G. Dworkin and Rosalind J. Dworkin (eds.), *The Minority Report,* third edition (New York: Harcourt Brace College Publishers, 1999)

10 The racism underlying these physical barriers have assumed the most blatant and crude forms. In late October 2000, for instance, the Village of Sauget, Illinois, set up a barricade of sawhorses and rocks on a major roadway connecting it to adjacent East St. Louis, a largely Black city. Local officials explained it as an attempt to stop speeders; yet this reasoning did not account for why leaders in predominantly white Sauget chose to prevent traffic from East St. Louis altogether. Black East St. Louis motorists had used the road as a thoroughfare to nearby shopping centers and workplaces. Unfortunately for them, several prominent Sauget residents (including the mayor, police, and fire chief) live along this route, and most likely did not like the idea of working-class Black people trafficking through "their" community. See George Pawlaczyk, "Barricade is Racially Motivated, Some Say," *Belleville News-Democrat,* October 26, 2000; and Doug Moore, "Blocked Road in Sauget Draws Complaints," *St. Louis Post-Dispatch,* November 5, 2000, D1-D6.

11 Mary Patillo-McCoy, *Black Picket Fences: Privilege and Peril Among the Black Middle-Class* (University of Chicago Press, 1999)

12 See Adolph Reed, Jr.'s "False Prophet" series on Louis Farrakhan in *The Nation:* "The Rise of Louis Farrakhan," January 21, 1991, 1, 51-56; and "All for One and None for All," January 28, 1991, 86-92. See also Barbara Ransby, "The Black Poor and the Politics of Expendability," *Race & Class,* Vol. 38, No. 2 (1996): 1-12.

13 Donna Ladd, "The Black Radical Congress Calls for Action: Forty Acres and One Big Digital Mule," *Village Voice,* January 10-16, 2001.

14 Hamer, "Rape and Race in the 21st Century," *The Final Call,* Sundiata Keita Cha-Jua, "*Slavery, Racist Violence, American Apartheid: The Case for Reparations,*" *New Politics,* Vol 8, No. 3 (Summer 2001): 46-64; and Neville and Hamer,

"'We Make Freedom,'" *Journal of Black Studies*. See also Manning Marable, "A Plea That Scholars Act Upon, Not Just Interpret, Events," *New York Times*, April 4, 1998, A13-15; and Jeff Sharlet, "Taking Black Studies Back to the Streets," *Chronicle of Higher Education*, May 19, 2000, A18-20.

15 Nellie Bailey, "Citywide Tenant Group Protests Gentrification," *BRC Today*, Vol. I, Issue 4 (Winter 2000-01): 4.

16 This project was conceived as an anthology on the scale of W.E.B. DuBois' Atlanta Studies and the National Urban League's *State of Black America* report. It aimed to present radical analyses of the contemporary role, position, and status of Black people in the US political economy, state, and civil society since 1975. The project was scheduled for completion in 2000. While it received formal endorsement by the BRC's National Council, the project withered due to a lack of support by several contributors, and general indifference.

17 On June 20, 2000, 150 members of the predominantly Black International Longshoremen Association, Local 1422, carried out a legal informational picket at the Port of Charleston, South Carolina. They were protesting the use of a non-union stevedoring company to unload the freighter of a union-busting Danish shipping line. The picket ended when participants clashed with 600 riot police following an attack on local president Kenneth Riley. In the aftermath of the confrontation, state attorney General Charles Condon sought felony charges against several union members. Five Black men were indicted on charges of rioting and conspiring to riot, and placed under house arrest pending trial. Freedom of association, economic justice for African Americans, and police terrorism were among the concerns that galvanized an international defense behind the "Charleston Five." Just before their scheduled trial date on November 13, 2001, this campaign, of which the BRC was part, forced the state attorney general to withdraw any felony charges and lift the union members from house arrest. The five defendants pled no contest to reduced misdemeanor charges and paid a token fine of $100.00 each. See Joann Wypijewski, "Audacity on Trial," *The Nation*, August 6, 2001; and Clarence Lang, "Freedom for the Charleston Five!" *BRC Today*, Vol. 1, Issue 4 (Winter 2000-01): 13-14. http://www.charlestonfivedefense.org.

18 Leah Samuel, "Thanks, BRC! We Needed That!" *BRC Today*, Vol. I, Issue 3 (Summer 2000): 1-

19 Abdul Alkalimat, "BRC Cyber Organizing: A Toledo Proposal," *BRC Today*, Vol. I, Issue 3 (Summer 2000): 4-5.

20 At age 21, New York City welfare recipient Tabitha Walrond, went on trial for the murder of her infant son, accused of deliberately starving him. Walrond consistently breastfed the baby, but because of an earlier surgery, was unable to produce sufficient nutrition. As the child's health deteriorated, she sought medical care for him on several occasions but her Medicaid HMO rejected her because the baby's card had not arrived yet. The card arrived in the mail several days after the baby's death. Advocates of welfare and women's rights, and BRC feminists, argued this was a clear consequence of

New York's welfare policies. Efforts to achieve the goals of the Personal Responsibility, Work, Opportunity, and Reconciliation Act and TANF have made it more difficult for the poor to obtain and sustain necessary benefits such as food stamps and Medicaid. See "HMO Kills Baby, Mother Convicted, Hospital Turns Poor Mother Away Twice," BRC press release, June 23, 1999.

21   In the realm of international affairs, one leading BRC member, Bill Fletcher, Jr., was part of a high-profile delegation that traveled to Cuba and met with president Fidel Castro. The group, assembled by Randall Robinson—head of the Washington, D.C. organization TransAfrica—was part of a public appeal to lift the US economic blockade against the island nation. In August 2001, many more BRC members attended the historic World Conference Against Racism in Durban, South Africa.

22   Jennifer Hamer, "The BRC Campaign: We Must Succeed," *BRC Today*, Vol. 1, Issue 4 (Winter 2000-01): 1-3.

23   Jennifer Hamer, "Black Radical Congress Today," *The Black World Today*, July 7, 2000. http://www.tbwt.com.

24   Hayward Horton et. al, "Lost in the Storm: The Sociology of the Black Working Class, 1850-1990," *American Sociology Review*, Vol. 65, No. 1 (February 2000): 128-137.

25   Hamer, "Black Radical Congress Today" and Sundiata Cha-Jua, Jennifer Hamer, Clarence Lang and Helen Neville, and "Being More Concrete," internal BRC position paper, July 19, 2000. See also John Woodford, "We're Not Overcoming (But We're Breathing Hard)," *The Black Scholar*, Vol. 28, No. 3-4 (Fall-Winter 1998): 2-7.

26   Cha-Jua, et. al., "Being More Concrete."

27   On April 7, 2001, nineteen-year-old Timothy Thomas was shot while fleeing police. The officers were pursuing the young Black male over warrants for a variety of minor misdemeanor violations, including not wearing a seat belt. Thomas was the 15th African American killed by Cincinnati police since January 1995. Segments of the city were placed under curfew during the several days of rioting that followed the incident. "Despite Report After Report, Unrest Endures in Cincinnati," Kevin Sack, *New York Times*, April 16, 2001, 1A; Susan Vela "Officer Shoots, Kills Suspect," *Cincinnati Enquirer*, April 8, 2001; and "Protest Spills into the Streets," *Cincinnati Post*, April 10, 2001.

28   The International Criminal Court (ICC) is a permanent court capable of investigating and bringing to justice states and individuals who commit serious violations of international humanitarian laws—specifically war crimes, crimes against humanity, genocide, and crimes of aggression. See *ICC Update*, twenty-seventh edition (New York, May 2002)

29   "USA PATRIOT" is an acronym for "Uniting and Strengthening America by Providing Appropriate Tools Required to Intercept and Obstruct Terrorism." The act created a broad definition of terrorist activities and domestic terrorism. Among other provisions, it allows the US Attorney General to incarcerate and detain non-citizens based on suspicion, and expands the ability of the government agencies to conduct secret searches and telephone and internet surveillance. The act also empowers the State Department and Department of Justice to designate domestic groups as terrorist organizations. Senator Russ Feingold, the only senator to oppose the bill, argued that the Act was reminiscent of earlier Alien and Sedition acts during World War I, the internment of Japanese-Americans during the Second World War, and the surveillance of antiwar protestors during the Vietnam era. President George W. Bush signed the bill into law on October 26, 2001. In May 2002, George W. Bush signed into law the Enhanced Border Security and Visa Entry Reform Act. The bill provides for 200 new investigators and 200 new inspectors for the Immigration and Naturalization Services (INS). It also requires foreign visitors to carry tamper resistant passports and documents that enable visitors to be identified through biometrics. The law requires the INS to establish a system that tracks the visas and enrollments of foreign students. See Carla Baranauckas, "Bush Signs Bill to Tighten Security at Nation's Borders," *New York Times,* May 14, 2002. See also Matthew Rothschild, "The New McCarthyism," *The Progressive,* January 2002, 18-23.

30 The Presidential Records Act of 1978 deemed the papers of out-going US presidents as public property. President George W. Bush's Executive Order 13233, signed in November 2001, requires archivists to notify former and incumbent presidents when they receive requests to examine records. Both are allowed to decide whether or not to claim "executive privilege" against the viewing of the respective documents. In cases where former presidents were deceased, surviving family members can decide on public access. The order also extends these privileges to the papers of vice presidents. Other evidence of the trend toward secrecy is George W. Bush's move to place his Texas governor papers in the library of his father George Bush, rather than in a state-run institution where they would be more accessible to the public.

31 In February 2002, the US General Accounting Office (GAO) filed an unprecedented federal court suit against Vice President Dick Cheney's refusal to hand over documents related to the development of national energy policy. The office was attempting to gain access to records of Cheney's private meetings with the heads of Enron and other energy firms to determine if any illegalities occurred. The George W. Bush Administration maintained that the GAO has no right to notes recorded during policy deliberation meetings between Cheney's energy task force, the energy industry, labor unions, or environmentalists. See Don Van Natta, Jr., "Agency Files Suit for Cheney Papers on Energy Policy," *New York Times,* February 23, 2002, 1A.

32 Feroz Ahmad, "The Historical Background to the Events of September 11, 2001, *Radical Historians Newsletter,* No. 85 (December 2001): 1-16; the Center for Political Education, "Questions & Answers about the War on Terrorism," www.politicaleducation.org; and Thomas Harrison, "Only a

Democratic Foreign Policy Can Combat Terrorism," *New Politics,* Vol. 8, No. 4 (Winter 2002): 23-42.

33   Hamer, "Black Radical Congress Today"; Cha-Jua, et. al., "Being More Concrete."

34   Cha-Jua, et. al., "Being More Concrete."

35   Ibid.

36   Many of those leveling the charge of sectarianism have had, at the back of their mind, the fractitious "Marxist/Nationalist" debates of the 1970s, which split Black united front organizations like the Congress of Afrikan Peoples, African Liberation Support Committee, and National Black Political Assembly. For background on this topic, see Manning Marable, "Black Nationalism in the 1970s: Through the Prism of Race and Class," *Socialist Review,* Vol. 10, No. 2-3 (March-June 1980): 57-109; Rod Bush, *We Are Not What We Seem: Black Nationalism and Class Struggle in the American Century* (New York University Press, 1999), 209-213; and Paul Costello, "A Critical History of the New Communist Movement, 1969-1979," *Theoretical Review* 13 (November-December 1979): 3-18. One may also consult the number of exchanges that unfolded on the pages of *The Black Scholar* between the July-August 1973 and March 1975 issues, including Haki R. Madhubuti, "The Latest Purge: The Attack on Black Nationalism and Pan-Afrikanism by the New Left, the Sons and Daughters of the Old Left," *The Black Scholar,* Vol. 6, No. 1 (September 1974): 43-56; and Mark Smith, "A Response to Haki Madhubuti," *The Black Scholar,* Vol. 6, No. 5 (January-February 1975): 44-53.

37   See "Corporate Imperialism vs. Black Liberation" in Robert L. Allen, *Black Awakening in Capitalist America: An Analytic History* (Trenton, N.J.: Africa World Press, 1990), 193-245; and the "Preface" to James Forman's political autobiography, *The Making of Black Revolutionaries* (Seattle: University of Washington Press, 1985).

Chapter 12

Towards the Black Radical Congress

Manning Marable

This article originally appeared in the Summer 1998 issue of
ColorLines.

For over a year, several hundred Black activists across the
country have been discussing the state of the African American freedom movement. The purpose of these discussions has
been to attempt to consolidate various constituencies and
groups within what could be called the Black left, into a single,
national political project.

This coordinated effort, called the Black Radical Congress
(BRC), convenes for the first time in Chicago from June 19–21,
1998. The BRC has the potential to become an important ideological and political pole in public policy debates inside the African
American community. But whether it fulfills its promise will depend on whether its participants learn from recent history and express their ideas and policies in a way that is both accessible to and
resonant with Black America.

Roots of the Black Radical Congress

Several important events prefigured the development of the
BRC. A decade ago, Jesse Jackson mounted an impressive national
campaign for the Democratic presidential nomination, receiving
over seven million popular votes. The Rainbow Coalition was on
the verge of becoming the most significant left-of-center force in

national politics with a presence both inside and outside the Democratic Party.

But following the 1988 election, Jackson decided—for reasons known only to himself—to dismantle his own organization. The radical wing of the Rainbow Coalition, which was already demoralized by the collapse of socialism, became increasingly fragmented. By the early and mid-1990s, the decline of the Rainbow left a gaping political vacuum, and various forces within the Black community attempted to fill it.

Two efforts were particularly significant. In 1994, the newly appointed national secretary of the NAACP, Benjamin Chavis, initiated a call for a national summit to a broad spectrum of Black organizations and representatives. These ranged from Kweisi Mfume, then head of the Congressional Black Caucus, to Nation of Islam leader Louis Farrakhan. Chavis' controversial ouster as NAACP national secretary halted the Summit's development.

Farrakhan then stepped forward in 1995 with a call for a Million Man March on Washington, DC. The program for the March was deeply problematic, with its emphasis on "atonement" and its misogynist orientation. Nevertheless, the Million Man March of October 16, 1995, was the largest public gathering of people of African descent in US history, and an inspiration to many more.

Still, despite the efforts of some progressive March organizers, Farrakhan and his reactionary entourage (which by that time included Chavis) failed to consolidate a secular or political infrastructure capable of mobilizing the Black masses. Farrakhan further reduced his credibility with his subsequent political affiliations with conservative white Republicans and cult leader Lyndon LaRouche.

Black leftists were bitterly divided in their assessments of the Million Man March. But despite these differences, nearly all agreed that a radical presence in national African American politics had completely disappeared.

Black Activists Organize

In the aftermath of the Million Man March, a number of Black leftists and activists initiated local discussion groups and networks. Agenda 2000 was formed in late 1995 by a prominent group of

Black feminists who publicly criticized the march. In Chicago, activists established the Ida B. Wells discussion group, named for the militant 19th-century feminist and journalist. In New York, the Ida B. Wells–W.E.B. DuBois Network was formed: a collective of Black writers, scholars, and activists who met monthly and sponsored public forums and projects.

In this context, five individuals with long histories of Black activism began to have discussions about the future of the Black left: Barbara Ransby, Abdul Alkalimat, Bill Fletcher, Leith Mullings, and myself. We come from diverse political backgrounds and organizational affiliations: democratic socialism, Marxism-Leninism, radical feminism, left-wing trade unionism. We saw in our ideological diversity the possibility of bringing together others who shared our disparate histories and experiences.

On March 1, 1997, the five of us convened an informal summit in Chicago of 35 people from around the country to discuss what to do. Participants included long-time political activists General Baker, Jarvis Tyner, and Jerome Scott; radical scholars Cornel West, Adolph Reed, Rose Brewer, Bill Strickland, and Cathy Cohen; and radical journalists Salim Muwakkil, Herb Boyd, and Lou Turner.

We all agreed that a national conference of Black radicals should be held. We concurred that we should not attempt to establish a new political organization, but instead find ways to encourage coalition building and joint activities among existing groups. To define the ideological ballpark for participation and working relationships, a Principles of Unity statement was adopted. By unanimous vote, we agreed to call this new project the Black Radical Congress (BRC). Everyone who attended the Chicago meeting became members of what was called the National Continuations Committee, and the five original conveners (Ransby, Alkalimat, Fletcher, Mullings, and myself) were named the BRC Coordinating Committee.

In May 1997, an expanded National Continuations Committee decided to hold the Black Radical Congress in Chicago on June 19, 1998. The date was selected for its historical symbolism, as "Juneteenth" marks the end of slavery in parts of the South. By

December, local organizing committees (LOCs) had been established in Chicago and New York. LOCs have also been initiated or planned in the San Francisco Bay Area, Los Angeles, Raleigh-Durham, Washington D.C., Cleveland, St. Louis, Philadelphia, and Detroit. To date, about 250 people have actively participated in BRC national and local meetings.

The New York Committee has been involved in several public demonstrations and planned several large public events of its own, including a political and cultural event marking the centennial of the birth of Paul Robson, held on May 1 at the Schomburg Center. Feminist scholars and activists Cathy Cohen and Lynette Jackson have been instrumental in building a BRC Feminist Caucus, with members drawn from throughout the country. A BRC Youth Caucus has also been established.

Fighting the Right

The process of mobilizing for a national Congress has not always been smooth. The BRC project brings together individuals and formations with distinctly different backgrounds, ideological orientations, and constituencies. Members have exchanged sharp words over issues such as homophobia and the practical and theoretical connections between race, gender, sexuality, and class. Nevertheless, all of us recognize that we cannot successfully oppose the right in this country unless we construct a strong progressive movement with grassroots militancy.

Central to this larger left project is the consolidation of the Black left. In some modest respects, this effort parallels the early development of the Congress of Racial Equality (CORE) in 1941, or the emergence in 1960 of the Student Nonviolent Coordinating Committee (SNCC) during the sit-in struggles across the South. The BRC should be understood as a transitional vehicle, an organizational expression of a collective effort by African-American activists to reestablish a militant protest movement that fights for social justice and progressive change.

New protest formations develop when established organizations fail to provide adequate leadership to meet new events and challenges. The socioeconomic crisis within the African American community today—widespread unemployment, the incarceration of almost an entire generation of young people, the collapse of human services programs, inadequate shelter and public health—provides the context for new forms of struggle.

Paths for the Future

The goal of Congress organizers is to bring 1,000 to 1,500 participants to Chicago on the June 19–21 weekend, with at least 350 low-income and working people busing in from New York City alone.

What will happen with the BRC after June 19? The BRC may adopt a Black Freedom Agenda, now in draft, which could provide a framework for continuing work around particular issues at both a local and national level. Several potentially important new national networks and projects are being developed. The Black Feminist Caucus brings together theorists like Barbara Smith with community activists. The Youth Caucus could be developed into a nationwide Black youth organization. Another possibility is a BRC-sponsored summer institute that brings together African American activists from community-based, women's, and labor organizations for classes in organizing techniques, tactics, and strategies.

Chapter 13

The Modern Struggle for Reparations

Johnita Scott-Obadele

In 1865, after nearly 200 years of legalized slavery, more than four million former slaves were set adrift with a safety net constructed only of paper.[1] Despite the promises of the US government—the guarantee of "forty acres and a mule" to each freed slave was perhaps the most famous broken pledge—there was no compensation for the centuries of unpaid labor. There was no "severance pay" to ease this immense and difficult transition.

Forbidden by law to read, these formerly enslaved people were sent forth without food or shelter to live among white people who had been taught that Blacks were inferior, depraved, and subhuman. Furthermore, Southern whites had lost a war and a way of life, and were more than ready to vent their anger and frustration. Not surprisingly, their targets were the mainly defenseless Black people in their midst.

After emancipation, Black people found themselves living with the lingering injuries of slavery and daily insults from America's "real citizens." The insults soon became institutionalized into oppressive laws that relegated Black people to an underclass, and gave local and state government the legal tools to keep them there.

Even in the face of overwhelming hostility, Black people were determined to carve a niche for themselves. Among their ranks were those who had served in the Union Army. There were also skilled and semiskilled craftspersons, blacksmiths, carpenters, equipment maintenance men, seamstresses, cooks, nurses, and horse trainers. They would attempt to use these skills to earn a living. The United States's answer to this notion of self-help was to allow and encourage a flood of European immigrants to dilute the need for Black labor and reduce the Black/white ratio. Poverty, lack of education, and even a criminal past did not prevent these "new Americans" from enjoying benefits that were withheld from Blacks. Soon the newcomers organized into restrictive and powerful trade unions controlling who worked in certain occupations and who was to be excluded. White citizens groups formed to enforce severe limitations on any movement that Black people made towards social, political, or economic parity.

This was the setting in which the National Ex-Slave Mutual Relief, Bounty, and Pension Association of the United States was established in 1894, led by Mrs. Callie House and Rev. Isaiah Dickerson. The sole purpose of the association was to get the United States to pay a small pension to those individuals still living who had previously been enslaved. This was 30 years after the Civil War, and many of the people who had come out of slavery were getting on in years, unable to work, and in dire need of assistance. The association collected dues to help finance the lobbying effort and a lawsuit that was filed on behalf of those once held in slavery. Instead of addressing in even a token way the past and ongoing injustices and crimes against Black people, the various governmental entities spent about 20 years observing and investigating, finding that the leaders had committed no crime. Even so, in 1916, mail fraud charges were brought against Mrs. House and she was convicted and sent to jail.[2]

The United States had brazenly used its might to break a grassroots movement that in no way threatened its sovereignty; a movement that asked for a small measure of justice and fair treatment.

At the time of Mrs. House's conviction, an extremely hostile climate prevailed in the United States for Black people. Court cases gave the green light to persecution, and oppression of the lowest order became commonplace. Voting rights had almost disappeared in some states. Lynching was becoming a participatory and spectator sport akin to the blood sports of ancient Europe.

With the demise of the National Ex-Slave Mutual Relief,

Bounty, and Pension Association, very little organized effort devoted to the issue of reparation for Black people in the United States—despite the singular cry issued by the venerable Queen Mother Moore in the early 1950s—is documented until the 1980s. Reparations did, however, appear either directly or conceptually on a list of programs and goals of many groups including the Nation of Islam, the Provisional Government of the Republic of New Afrika, the Self-Determination Committee, the National Black United Front, the Urban League, the National Association for the Advancement of Colored People (NAACP), and many others. Reparation demands were also contained in the Black Manifesto adopted in 1969 by the National Black Economic Development Conference. Perhaps there was never a time during our period of enslavement and afterwards, when someone was not writing, speaking, or at least thinking about what this country owes us and how we could collect.

Yet reparations efforts on behalf of Black people were scattered and fragmented. There were occasional publications, speeches here and there, individual appeals, organizational resolutions, and aggreived references to "forty acres and a mule," but no group had taken on the challenge of pushing for a reparations law—it was not recognized as a national, political issue. By the 1980s, some forward-thinking activists realized that, even though they were members and even leaders of groups promoting reparations, the best chance of winning reparations was through a unified but focused push. These long-time civil and human rights activists formed the National Coalition of Blacks for Reparations in America (N'COBRA) in 1987.

The First Modern Grassroots Reparations Organization

Although N'COBRA was the vision of the Republic of New Afrika (RNA) and the National Conference of Black Lawyers, membership in the coalition was open to anyone interested in the issue. The mission was, and still is, to make the demand for reparations a national priority and international issue. As stated in its bylaws:

The Coalition is to serve as a coordinating body for the reparation effort in America; to develop unified goals and strategies to win reparations; to disseminate and exchange information on reparations issues important to Africans everywhere; and to educate the general public about the just demand for reparations.[3]

N'COBRA held its first town meeting in Washington, DC in April 1989. Massachusetts state representative Bill Owens, who had introduced a reparations bill in his state legislature, was the featured speaker. Later that year, N'COBRA hosted its first annual national conference. Members of the organization discussed a draft bill calling for reparations, prepared by Congressman John Conyers, with the congressman's staff. The bill, titled "a Commission to Study Reparations Proposals for African Americans Act" and assigned the number H.R. 3745, was first introduced in the House of Representatives in the 101st Congress, November 20, 1989.

While it has been repeatedly tabled, Congressman Conyers has reintroduced his bill in every subsequent Congress. N'COBRA agreed that the coalition should publicize and lobby on behalf of the bill which called on the United States to:

[A]cknowledge the fundamental injustice, cruelty, brutality, and inhumanity of slavery in the United States and the 13 American colonies between 1619 and 1865 and to establish a commission to examine the institution of slavery, subsequent de jure and de facto racial and economic discrimination against African Americans, and the impact of these forces on living African Americans, to make recommendations to the Congress on appropriate remedies, and for other purposes.[4]

Since its founding, N'COBRA has produced periodic newsletters, an annual magazine, and conducted national conventions. Its website (www.ncobra.com) is a useful resource for activists interested in reparations efforts taking place across the country. N'COBRA established Reparations Awareness Day in 1993. And since 1993, every February the organization has sponsored public reparations programs in various US communities around the country.

N'COBRA bylaws promote broad participation—national

membership is estimated in the thousands—and keep the organization diverse, representative, and balanced. For example, dues are low (ten dollars for individuals, twenty-five dollars and fifty dollars respectively for local and national organizations.) Prisoners who wish to join the organization can have their fee waived.

Furthermore, there are numerous indications that some of our most important institutions are not working optimally because of a lack of female/male balance and sexist practices. N'COBRA by-laws require male and female co-chairs of the Coalition. Co-chairs are limited to three consecutive terms (six years). This insures fresh leadership so the issue, not an individual, remains the "star." Dispersed rather than concentrated leadership is a reason that N'COBRA has been able to soften the climate so that a reasoned discussion of reparations can take place.

Why Reparations Now?

Those of us who work for reparations are often asked why we are digging up the past. Some say that slavery happened so many years ago and it's too late to do anything about it now. A favorite argument is that all victims and perpetrators of the horrific acts associated with slavery are long dead, consequently, there is no one who rightly owes and no one who has a right to collect. Some critics even suggest that the United States has properly atoned and made amends for the past through the institution of various welfare programs, affirmative action, and civil rights legislation.

Yet, what happened in the past has direct and indirect influence on the quality of our lives today. Over the space of several centuries, America built up a huge debt with its Black population. The enslavement of Africans quickly yielded wealth and prosperity for the colonies that became the United States. This young nation's might soon exceed that of other countries with ancient and glorious histories. The involuntary servitude of our ancestors was perhaps the single most important factor in this rapid accumulation of power. Their unpaid labor laid the foundation.

If the US government had provided even a measure of justice to the five million freed slaves in 1865, there would be no grounds for their 35 million descendants to stake a demand. Debt increases in amount and complexity when not paid on time. Obligations are not dismissed because a debtor successfully uses delaying tactics to avoid paying. Debt does not cease to exist with the demise of the primary parties. Even if death did in fact dismiss debt, the parties involved are the United States and Black people. Both are alive.

Slavery ended in 1865, but vestiges of this abominable system clearly remained until the civil rights laws of the 1960s were passed. One hundred years after the Civil War, the people whose labor had built a mighty and wealthy nation, whose talent had uplifted and entertained, whose courage had turned the tide in military conflicts, had to take to the streets and the courts to obtain the most basic human rights. These rights included access to public restrooms and eating and sleeping facilities, the right to vote, to obtain health care, to attend certain state universities, and to sit in any vacant bus seat after purchasing a ticket. After the laws were in place, they had to be tested. This ushered in a period of death and terror for Blacks and their allies, which made the 1960s and the 1970s bear close resemblance to the 1860s and the 1870s.

For the injured party, reparation represents respect. There is an unquenchable need to have an injustice acknowledged and compensated. For Black people, reparations would recognize our unique role in this country's history.

Reparation means resources. US census information reminds us that the income gap between Blacks and whites is still wide. We are woefully lagging in business ownership and control of financial institutions. Since wealth (and poverty) is passed from one generation to another, what each generation starts with is more or less based on what occurred in the preceding one. And, in every region of this country, discrimination prevented the great majority Blacks from having certain jobs, no matter what qualifications they possessed. This guaranteed that the majority of Blacks would live on less than whites, and have less money to leave for their heirs. A game of "catch up" is impractical and almost impossible when you have been unpaid and underpaid for multiple generations.

We heap criticism on each other for not shopping and investing in our own communities. While these efforts are useful, we must not embrace the popular lie that we are in our present economic condition because we are not smart enough or don't work hard enough. Working harder and spending wiser are important and helpful to everybody but to think that they will bring us collective economic equality is a myth. In terms of income and wealth, Blacks still lag far behind whites.[5] This fact will not be altered by our constant talk about the vast amount of money passing through our communities. In matters related to money and wealth, the damage caused by centuries of deprivation are undeniable. Reparations are needed to bridge a gap we did not make.

Past government attempts to invest in the Black community have had very limited positive results. The main reason is that Black people never had any autonomy in exercising control over the programs. There were lots of strings and some of them seemed to have no purpose except to entangle and hang well-meaning program administrators. We need to be able to determine how we will use resources that are released to us.

And for any payment to be reparations, it must be called by its proper name. Welfare, block grants, wars on poverty, and other forms of aid are not synonyms for reparations. Any deserving citizen can benefit from these government-sponsored projects. That's why affirmative action seemed to promise the greatest opportunites for access and economic advancement. Quotas and set-asides finally created opportunities for Black contractors and small business owners. Large corporations and universities attempted to prove their openness to Blacks who had historically been excluded. Some offered special scholarships and recruitment incentives as expressions of their sincerity.

But just as policy and practice were coming together to afford Black people broader opportunities, successful judicial attacks were launched. The Bakke decision, the Adarand decision, and a series of state and local propositions and lawsuits made affirmative action just another example of America's crooked dealing with Black people by giving in one breath and taking back in the next. And vowing to end affirmative action became a way of getting elected to public office. Black people were once again forced to fight for the right to hold certain jobs and to attend institutions that were being financed by our tax dollars. Even some Black people who had experienced firsthand the value of affirmative action felt compelled to speak out against it for political expediency and gain.

So, why a modern-day fight for reparations? The civil rights movement won crucial human rights and political advances in the area of elective politics, but there is unfinished business between the United States and its Black population. Black people know we have been seriously wronged—economically, culturally, psychically—by slavery, and the next logical next step in our struggle for respect and equality is to attempt to correct the historical equation.

What the Future Holds

And the fight for reparations, powered by activists at the grassroots level, is gaining steam. At the historic World Conference Against Racism in 2001 in Durban, South Africa, the international slave trade was recognized as a crime against humanity.[6]

In 2002, Councilman Charles Barron of New York City introduced a bill in the City Council for reparations and similar legislative acts have been launched in Vermont and New Hampshire.[7]

In 2002, Roger Wareham of the Brooklyn-based December 12th Movement filed the first federal class-action lawsuit demanding reparations from three major corporations—FleetBoston, Aetna, and CSX. The lawsuit, on behalf of 35 million descendants, seeks compensation from a number of defendants for profits earned through slave labor and the slave trade. [8]

And following the lead of N'COBRA, other reparations groups like the December 12th Movement have formed in the last few years.

Randall Robinson, former director of TransAfrica and author of *The Debt* and *The Reckoning,* and Harvard Law School professor Charles Ogletree co-chair the Reparations Coordinating Committee. The Reparations Coordinating Committee will soon be filing its own reparations lawsuit.

In his book *The Reckoning,* Robinson observes:

> Were we to receive $10 trillion tomorrow and we had not ourselves taken collateral measures to repair the psychological injury that we have sustained during the long, unremitting onslaught, the money would do us no lasting benefit. After a de-

cades-long campaign waged in a court of legal opinion, we may well receive for our pains a measure of material recompense. But little else in the way of comfort should be hoped for from a nation that perpetrated against us the longest-running crime against humanity known to the world over the last five hundred years.[9]

In fact, we often hear the word "impossible" when we use "Black people" and "reparations" in the same sentence. I will close with a quote from noted writer/activist James Baldwin:

I know that what I am asking is impossible. But in our time, as in every time, the impossible is the least one can demand—and one is, after all, emboldened by the spectacle of human history in general and American Negro history in particular, for it testified to nothing less than the perpetual achievement of the impossible.[10]

1   For information on the importance of June 1865, see
http://www.elecvillage.com/juneteen.htm and http://rs6.loc.gov/
ammem/alhtml/almtime.html.

2   The information about the National Ex-Slave Mutual Relief, Bounty and
Pension Association came from the unpublished work of the late Chris
Alston of Detroit; and Mary Frances Berry, "Reparations for Freedmen,
1890-1916: Fraudulent Practices or Justice Deferred?," *Journal of Negro
History* 57, no. 3 (July 1972): 219-230.

3   For more information, contact National Coalition of Blacks for
Reparations in America (N'COBRA), P.O. Box 90604, Washington, D.C.
20090-0604. http://www.ncobra.com.

4   *A Commission to Study Reparations Proposals for African Americans Act*, 101st
Cong., US House of Representatives,. 3745.

5   See Julianne Malveaux, "Still at the Periphery: The Economic Status of
African-Americans," *Race and Resistance: African-Americans in the Twenty-First
Century* (Cambridge: South End Press, 2002).

6   Office of the United Nations High Commissioner for Human Rights,
*Report of the World Conference against Racism, Racial Discrimination, Xenophobia
and Related Intolerance* (Geneva: United Nations, January 2002). For more
information on the Conference, see http://www.racism.gov.za.

7   See http://www.council.nyc.ny.us.

8   See http://www.december12thmovement.bigstep.com.

9   Randall N. Robinson, *The Reckoning: What Blacks Owe to Each Other* (New
York: E. P. Dutton, 2002).

10   James Baldwin, *The Fire Next Time* (New York: Vintage, 1992).

Chapter 14

In the Fight of Our Lives

Notes on the AIDS Crisis in the Black Community

Phill Wilson

On June 5, 1981, the Centers for Disease Control and Prevention (CDC) reported the first cases of what we know now as AIDS. In the first 20 years of the epidemic, more than 155,000 African American lives were lost to the disease.[1]

The latest AIDS statistics show the staggering toll of HIV/AIDS on people of African descent in the US. While Blacks represent around 12 percent of the total population, we account for 37.7 percent of the accumulated AIDS cases, and more than 50 percent of new AIDS cases.[2] In 2000, Black men made up 40 percent of the new AIDS cases among males; Black women represented 62 percent of reported AIDS cases among females; and 6.2 of every 10 children reported with AIDS in the US were Black.[3]

A CDC study of gay or bisexual men released in 2000 found that over 30 percent of the Black men in the study were already infected with HIV. Even more shocking, researchers discovered that the majority of these men were infected recently.[4]

The rapid spread of AIDS in the Black community is clearly related to our economic status and access to health care. Throughout the epidemic, African Americans have fared worse than whites and other groups on every health care measure: we are diagnosed later in the course of the disease, receive worse care, benefit last from new advances in treatment, and die faster.[5]

Major newspapers and magazines may be comfortable declaring, as some began to in the late 1990s, that we are in the twilight of the epidemic in the United States. Yet, the Centers for Disease Control (CDC) in Atlanta continue to report that infection rates remain steady, at best. Among African Americans, the infection rate continues to climb alarmingly.[6] AIDS is not over in Harlem, on Chicago's South Side, Watts, Detroit, or Macon, Georgia. And some would argue it's just beginning in Soweto, Nairobi, and Victoria Falls. Across the globe, Black people are on the Frontline of this pandemic. The reality is that class, gender, sexuality, and race do matter a great deal in this epidemic.

AIDS Policy and Public Health Questions

Policy-makers often seem at cross-purposes, and their efforts to prevent the spread of the virus and treat people living with AIDS are sometimes exacerbated by a lack of resources and understanding. Still, the answers to our survival in terms of our fight against the HIV epidemic will come from the questions and problems posed in the political and economic realities of the last decade. HIV other epidemics have revealed the frailty of our health care systems and the power of human indifference, prejudice, attitudes, morality, and greed in medical economics and access.

Yet, these lessons are not new. The epidemics of homelessness and drug and alcohol addiction still exist and their lessons have gone largely unheeded.

Twenty years ago, this country was well on its way toward the elimination of tuberculosis. With the onset of the HIV epidemic, funding was slowly and subtly redirected from TB control to HIV and now we face the greater challenges to control both infections.

Today, Hepatitis C is on the rise at a horrifying rate. Will we continue to address one at the cost of the other? Will we let political will and advocacy determine the winner? Or will we begin to see AIDS, Tuberculosis, Hepatitis, homelessness, drug and alcohol addiction, and urban violence within the context of a greater vision of community health?

Homophobia Kills

While the AIDS epidemic has certainly spread far beyond the gay community, homophobia within the Black community has stalled our response to the crisis, and is fueling the spread in our communities today.

Every day, Black men, women, teenagers, and babies are being infected, because homophobia creates a barrier that prevents us from developing and implementing effective strategies to fight HIV/AIDS. Black women continue to get infected at higher rates than white women, many of them by men who have been or are sexually active with other men.[7] Many of these men are very clear about their sexual orientation, but engage in relationships with women because they cannot bear the pressure from family, church, and friends.

Black teenagers have one of the highest rates of new HIV infections in the country. Teenagers feel there's no safe place for them, no home that will welcome their sexuality. Look at what the dominant culture teaches them—preachers still choose condemnation over education. Politicians still choose abdication over action. Entertainers still choose humiliation over recognition.

All of us as African Americans—male or female, openly gay or not—pay a price for that silence. Who among us doesn't have some part of our life we do on the "down low," or something that sets us apart? You may be shorter than normal, or fatter, or drink a little. Watching people be shunned for their "otherness," every one of us begins to feel a little doubt about ourselves. You want to deny that part of yourself that doesn't measure up, and not speak up. If we are serious about stopping AIDS, we have to end the silence and stigma around homosexuality—and in the process rethink our beliefs about what it means to be Black and male in America today.

And if we want to decrease the rate of HIV infection among African Americans, we need to increase the dialogue—not shut it down. For African American institutions, this means supporting visible gay Black leadership, and not just assuming that antigay prejudice is someone else's problem. For individual Black men, it means expanding the way we think—not just about straight and gay, but about the whole range of human possibilities. What does it say when it's okay for a young Black man to imagine himself as a rapper or athlete, but not as president of American Express, a Supreme Court Justice, or the next Alvin Ailey? Similarly, what do we get out of denying the diversity of sexual identity and behavior in our communities? How many more lives will such narrow definitions of masculinity cost us?

We must redefine Black masculinity. Many young Black men think that procreation is some kind of recreation; that making a baby is the same as raising a child. We must expand Black male role models beyond sports and music. We must value, grow, and support fathers. And we must teach our sons that condom use is their responsibility.

African American men are disproportionately represented among America's incarcerated population. These men often enter the penal system HIV-negative, but leave HIV-positive. And these men return to Black communities. Correctional health facilities must provide appropriate counseling and treatment to inmates, and help in integrating them back into society armed with the knowledge and skills to care for themselves and prevent further infections. We can raise awareness about the relationship between HIV and the criminal justice system.

Finally, we must confront stigma in our communities. In the face of derision, fear, and sometimes even hostility, Black people won't get tested and seek treatment for HIV. In the face of homophobia and antidrug hysteria, people are afraid to disclose their risk factors. People living with HIV/AIDS are an invaluable source of information and leadership in fighting the stigmas that perpetuate this disease. By sharing their stories, and giving a face to a nameless epidemic, they can inspire hope and promote prevention.

The Role of the Black Church

As an AIDS advocate, I am acutely aware of the walls we Black folks build to separate ourselves one from another. In the AIDS community, we build walls between those who were quick to mobilize and those who were slow to get involved, between those who want to be all inclusive and those who choose to address certain populations, walls between those comfortable with having frank and open discussions about sex and sexuality, and those who are uncomfortable, shy, or timid.

Many people believe that one of the root causes of the spread of HIV/AIDS in Black communities is homophobia in the Black church. A reporter recently asked me if attempting to get Black churches involved in efforts to fight HIV/AIDS is a waste of time and resources.

The Black church gets too much credit and too much blame for what is right and wrong in Black communities. Churches are among our oldest and most stable institutions, but they are not the only institutions in the Black community; and among certain segments of the community, they are not the most important or relevant institutions.

Still, Black churches are any more or less homophobic than any other churches. After all, it was not the our churches did not spawned Fred Phelps, Lou Sheldon, Pat Robertson, Franklin Graham, or Jerry Falwell. Some Black clergy have followed the lead of these right-wing demagogues. But the faith community can be an invaluable source of support in the fight against HIV/AIDS in African American communities.

Someday we will have to face the question, "What did your generation do about AIDS?" We have the tools to end this AIDS epidemic. The challenge is whether or not we have the moral will to use those tools effectively and compassionately.

We must encourage people to know their status. Voluntary HIV counseling and testing is the portal to HIV prevention and care. Being HIV-positive is no longer an automatic and immediate death sentence. There are treatments that slow disease progression and may also reduce the risk of transmitting the virus to others. But the benefits of treatment are unavailable to those who don't know they're infected.

We must advocate for access to free, anonymous, and voluntary HIV counseling and testing designed to meet the unique needs of African Americans.

We must help empower young women and girls. Young women must be taught how to protect themselves and be supported in saying no to unwanted sex. We must foster a culture that values women more.

We have the power to change the trajectory of the HIV/AIDS epidemic in our communities.

We're the ones we've been waiting for.

1   Centers for Disease Control and Prevention, *HIV/AIDS Surveillance Report,* Vol 12, No. 1, 2000.

2   Ibid.

3   Ibid.

4   Eighth Conference on Retroviruses and Opportunistic Infections, February 4-8, 2001, Chicago.

5   National Center of Health Statistics, *National Vital Statistics Reports,* Vol. 48, No. 11, July 24, 2000.

6   Centers for Disease Control, *HIV/AIDS Surveillance Report,* Vol. 12 No. 1, 2000.

7   For more information, see http://www.blackwomenshealth.com/ HIV_AIDS.

RESOURCES FOR PEOPLE WITH HIV/AIDS AND ALLIES

ACT UP/New York-AIDS Coalition to Unleash Power
ACT UP/New York
332 Bleecker Street, Suite G5
New York, NY 10014
212-966-4873 (phone)
actupny@panix.com (email)
http://www.actupny.org (website)

A diverse, non-partisan group of individuals united in anger and committed to direct action to end the AIDS crisis. Respond to action alerts through demonstrations, letter writing, and donations. Get information about starting or joining a local ACT UP chapter in your area.

African American AIDS Policy and Training Institute
1833 W. 8th Street, Suite 200
Los Angeles, CA 90057-4257
213-353-3610 (phone)
http://www.blackaids.org (website)

Dedicated to the fight against AIDS for people of African descent. Projects include the Simon Nkoli Exchange program, a "Peace Corps" type exchange program for US and African front-line HIV/AIDS workers. The Institute also sponsors training for peer treatment educators.

AIDS Action
1906 Sunderland Place, NW
Washington, DC 20036
202-530-8030 (phone)
http://www.aidsaction.org (website)

A network of 3200 AIDS service organizations across the country and the one million HIV-positive Americans they serve, dedicated solely to responsible federal policy for improved HIV/AIDS care and services, vigorous medical research, and effective prevention. Offers opportunities to get involved through the legislative action center, action alerts, and petitions.

AIDS Memorial Quilt
The NAMES Project Foundation AIDS Memorial Quilt
PO Box 5552
Atlanta, GA 31107
404-688-5500 (phone)
displays@aidsquilt.org (email)
http://www.aidsquilt.org/Newsite (website)

Largest, on-going community arts project in the world. The quilt provides a creative means for remembrance and healing, while increasing public awareness of AIDS. You can volunteer to help at a local chapter or to host a display in your community or school.

ARK of Refuge, Inc.
1025 Howard Street
San Francisco, CA 94103
415-861-6130 (phone)
info@arkofrefuge.org (email)
http://www.arkofrefuge.org (website)

The staff of The Ark of Refuge, Inc. has been working together since 1988 when they collectively designed a program, which became a Northern California model for promoting AIDS education in the African American community and targeted high-risk groups.

The Audre Lorde Project
85 South Oxford Street
Brooklyn, NY
718-596-1328
alpinfo@alp.org (email)
http://www.alp.org (website)

The Audre Lorde Project is a Lesbian, Gay, Bisexual, Two Spirit and Transgender People of Color center for community organizing, focusing on the New York City area. Through mobilization, education, and capacity-building, we work for community wellness and progressive social and economic justice. Committed to struggling across differences, we seek to responsibly reflect, represent, and serve our various communities.

Balm in Gilead
130 West 42nd Street, Suite 450
New York, NY 10036
212-730-7381 (phone)
info@balmingilead.org (email)
http://www.balmingilead.org (website)

A not-for-profit, non-governmental organization with an international mission to stop the spread of HIV/AIDS throughout the African Diaspora by building the capacity of faith communities to provide AIDS education and support networks for all people living and affected by HIV/AIDS .

Buddhist AIDS Project (BAP)
415-522-7473 (phone)
buddhistap@buddhistaidsproject.org (email)
http://www.buddhistaidsproject.org (website)

An all-volunteer, non-profit affiliate of the Buddhist Peace Fellowship (BPF), BAP serves anyone living with HIV/AIDS, including family, friends, caregivers and people who are HIV negative. Based in San Francisco, BAP also provides information about Buddhist teachings, practice centers, and special events. They also highlight current HIV/AIDS news, with links to local, national, and international resources.

Gay and Lesbian Medical Association
459 Fulton Street, Suite 107
San Francisco, California 94102
415-255-4547 (phone)
info@glma.org (email)
http://www.glma.org (website)

GLMA was founded in 1981 as the American Association of Physicians for Human Rights. GLMA promotes quality health care for LGBT and HIV-positive people, fosters a professional climate in which its diverse members can achieve their full potential, and supports members challenged by discrimination on the basis of sexual orientation.

Gay Men of African Descent
103 E. 125th Street, Suite 503
New York, NY 10035
212-414-9344 (phone)
gmad@aol.com (email)
http://www.gmad.org (website)

Assists community-based organizations in the Northeast with a special focus on African American gay men and community planning groups.

Harlem United
123-125 W. 124th Street
New York, NY
212-531-1300 (phone)
http://www.harlemunited.org/mission.html (website)

Provide quality HIV prevention and care services in a safe environment, while uniting the diverse communities of Harlem in order to address all needs of people living with and threatened by HIV and AIDS.

Minority AIDS Project
5149 W. Jefferson Boulevard
Los Angeles, CA 90016
323-936-4949 (phone)
http://members.aol.com/map5149/map.html (website)

MAP's mission is to reduce suffering and deaths due to HIV/AIDS in communities of color by making HIV/AIDS-related human services easily accessible and available to these communities and by designing preventive education programs that match the framework of their culture and their lives.

NAACP
4805 Mt. Hope Drive
Baltimore, MD 21215
877-NAACP-98 (toll-free phone)
410-521-4939 (NAACP 24 Hour Hotline)
http://www.naacp.org (website)

The NAACP works at the national, regional, and local level to secure civil rights through advocacy for supportive legislation and by the implementation of our Strategic Initiatives.

National Association of People With AIDS
1413 K Street, NW
Washington, DC 20005
202-898-0414 (phone)
napwa@napwa.org (email)
http://www.napwa.org (website)

NAPWA has been a strong and consistent national leader for people with AIDS, ensuring that a voice is always at the table when decisions affecting AIDS survivors' lives are being made.

The National Black Leadership Commission on AIDS
105 East 22nd Street, Suite 711
New York, NY 10010
212-614-0023 (phone)
info@blca.org (email)
http://www.blca.org (website)

BLCA conducts policy, research, and advocacy on HIV and AIDS to ensure effective participation of our leadership in all policy and resource allocation divisions at the national, state, and local levels of communities of African descent nationwide.

National Catholic AIDS Network
P.O. Box 422984
San Francisco, CA 94142-2984
707-874-3031 (phone)
info@ncan.org (email)
http://www.ncan.org (website)

National organization devoted exclusively to helping the Catholic Church respond in an informed and compassionate manner to the challenges presented by the HIV/AIDS pandemic. Provides educational materials for youths, individuals, and parishes about understanding AIDS and the Catholic Church. Also sponsors an online forum for spiritual discussions.

National Minority AIDS Council
1931 13th Street, NW
Washington, DC 20009
202-483-6622 (phone)
info@nmac.org (email)
http://www.nmac.org (website)

Dedicated to developing leadership within communities of color to address the challenges of HIV/AIDS by producing educational materials and sponsoring conferences. The website offers an HIV/AIDS job database and useful links to other organizations.

OutReach, Inc.
825 Cascade Avenue, SW
Atlanta, GA 30311
404-755-6700 (phone)
http://www.outreachatlanta.org (website)

The mission and purpose of OutReach is to provide culturally-sensitive AIDS and drug abuse education prevention programs to minority communities in Metropolitan Atlanta's inner-city neighborhoods and throughout the State of Georgia.

Rainbow/PUSH Coalition
930 East 50th Street
Chicago, IL 60615-2702
773-373-3366 (phone)
info@rainbowpush.org (email)
http://www.rainbowpush.org/ (website)

The National Rainbow/PUSH Coalition (RPC) is a multi-racial, multi-issue, international membership organization founded by Rev. Jesse L. Jackson, Sr. that is working to move the nation and the world toward social, racial and economic justice.

SisterLove, Inc.
PO Box 10558
1285-A Ralph David Abernathy Boulevard, SW
Atlanta, Georgia 30310
404-753-7733 (phone)
info@sisterlove.org (email)
http://www.sisterlove.org (website)

SisterLove is on a mission to eradicate the impact of HIV/AIDS and other reproductive health challenges upon women and their families through education, prevention, support and human rights advocacy in the United States and around the world.

Student Global AIDS Campaign (SGAC)
c/o Global Justice
30 Brattle Street, 4th floor
Cambridge, MA 02138
617-495-2090 (phone)
http://www.stopglobalaids.org (website)

Student network devoted to combating the global AIDS crisis and changing the US AIDS policy by drawing upon the passion of students. SGAC's work includes regional conferences, media outreach, and political advocacy. You can create or join an SGAC chapter at your school or university.

Chapter 15

George Bush's Global Agenda

Bad News for Africa

Salih Booker

A version of this essay appeared in the May 2001 issue of *Current History*.

The greatest international challenge facing the United States in the twenty-first century is to devise a strategy to overcome the world's structural inequities that perpetuate extreme poverty. In a world where race, place, class, and gender are the major determinants of people's access to the full spectrum of human rights needed to escape poverty, Africa should be at the top of the United States foreign policy agenda. In a way—albeit the wrong way—it already is.

To find the substance of United States foreign policy toward the nations and peoples of Africa, however, one must know where to look. During the tenure of the previous administration, it was necessary to see beyond the travel itineraries of cabinet secretaries and President Bill Clinton himself to the parsimonious management of the budget and the rising death toll from conflicts and AIDS to discern the yawning gap between rhetoric in Washington and reality in Africa. With the new administration it will be necessary to look past the conventional categories of what it will call Africa policy—conflict resolution, political reform, and economic and commercial relations—to the broader use of United States power in determining matters of global governance. Today's "global" issues, from HIV/AIDS to global warming, and from trade policies to the failure of international peacekeeping, have their most immediate and devastating consequences in Africa. And it is equally true that these vital challenges must be addressed in Africa, in solidarity with Africans, if they are not to overwhelm the world.

Africa policy is thus no longer to be found at the margins of United States global politics but in the mainstream. At present, however, this is bad news for Africa.

When the snowcaps of Mt. Kilimanjaro melt in a decade or two, the damage done by the real Africa policies of the world's sole superpower at the dawn of this new century will be manifest. The floods that have devastated Mozambique and many other southern African countries in the past two years are but omens of that future. Like the AIDS pandemic that is wreaking havoc on African societies and economies, global warming is also taking its toll primarily among poor countries in the South, mainly in Africa. These consequences are not merely the result of "natural" disasters compounded by neglect on the part of the richest country on earth. Rather they are the strange fruit of what amounts to years of aggressive and irresponsible behavior by the United States.

The National Interest

During the electoral campaign, George W. Bush and his advisers repeatedly stressed that Africa did not "fit into the national strategic interests" of America. During the televised presidential debates, he said Africa was not a priority, and that he would not intervene to prevent or stop genocide in Africa should such a threat—as occurred in Rwanda in 1994—develop. Since he took office, a few officials, Secretary of State Colin Powell most notable among them, have tried to amend this statement with reassurances that African concerns, such as AIDS, will be taken seriously by this administration.

Other Bush supporters have noted, correctly, that although the Clinton administration gave much attention to Africa, it was slow to deliver in practical terms. They hold out hope that Bush will promise less and deliver more. Thus far, the new administration has only promised a substantive Africa policy without revealing much in the way of details and taking no early positive actions.

A fundamental problem is that the team of President George Bush and Vice President Dick Cheney will, like all its predecessors, shape United States foreign policy based on its own version of the national interest. At times, the administration will slant it to concentrate on strategic or security interests. At other moments, economic interests will get top billing. And, on some occasions, political interests, even values, will be put forward as the core of the national interest. But all of these interpretations of the national interest will share limitations that stem from the exclusion of those most affected—Africans.

The net effect of the administration's broader policies already amount to a de facto war on Africa. Consider President Bush's decision to not seek reductions in carbon dioxide emissions—as he had explicitly promised he would during the electoral campaign. Media commentators quickly noted how the move would arouse criticism from domestic and European environmentalists and doom hopes of completing negotiations on the Kyoto Protocol, a treaty that would require signatory states to cut their greenhouse gas emissions—including carbon dioxide—below 1990 levels by the year 2012. Such gases are believed by most scientists to be responsible for the increased warming of the earth's atmosphere during the last century.

But few recalled the recent warning from Klaus Toepfer, executive director of the UN Environment Program, that Africa would suffer the most from the effects of global warming: "Africa's share of the global population is 14 percent but it is responsible for only 3.2 percent of global carbon dioxide emissions. Africans face the most direct consequences with regard to extreme weather conditions, with regard to drought and storms." Developed countries, principally the United States, produce the vast majority of the greenhouse gas emissions.

Just weeks before Bush's policy reversal, glaciologist Lonnie Thompson of Ohio State University released a study predicting that the glacier ice atop Mt. Kilimanjaro would disappear entirely between 2010 and 2020. And massive floods in Mozambique for the second consecutive year demonstrated the region's vulnerability to extreme weather, which global warming may exacerbate. A January report by the Intergovernmental Panel on Climate Change laid out a long list of predicted damage for Africa, ranging from water shortages and declines in food production to expanded ranges for malaria and other vector-borne diseases. The decision on carbon dioxide emissions makes the United States a rogue state, in global environmental terms, as far as Africans are concerned.

The War on Reproductive Health

George W. Bush's first full working day as president of the United States was also the twenty-eighth anniversary of *Roe v. Wade*, the Supreme Court decision that first established a woman's constitutional right to abortion. On that day, his first exercise of authority was to impose the contentious abortion politics of one narrow domestic constituency on millions of people in the poor countries of the world. By reinstating the "global gag rule"—slashing funding for family planning services overseas—Bush did not really intend to reduce the number of abortions; rather, his true purpose was to advance the ideological agenda of the antichoice religious fundamentalists who are among his strongest supporters.

The rule was first imposed by President Ronald Reagan in 1984, during a population conference in Mexico City. It was sustained by Bush's father, President George H.W. Bush, but reversed by President Bill Clinton in 1993. The measure (also known as the Mexico City Policy) denies federal funding to international organizations that provide public health and family-planning services if they also provide reproductive health education and abortion services through their own funds.

As a result of Bush's action, organizations delivering important health care assistance in Africa will lose funding. Projects providing contraceptives will be cut, which will contribute to a greater demand for abortions. More unsafe abortions will occur, as happened during the last period this policy was enforced. And with the decrease in the full range of family planning services, there will be an increase in the incidence of HIV/AIDS infections on a continent that is already experiencing unprecedented suffering and social destruction because of the AIDS pandemic.

Congresswoman Nita Lowey (D-NY) said the president was "declaring war on the reproductive health of the world's poorest women." When members of Congress from both parties moved to stop Bush, the White House announced that it would reissue the order through an executive memorandum, which is not subject to congressional review. The unseemly rush to reimpose the gag rule offers evidence of just how antagonistic the Bush administration is to the interests of poor people, especially Black people. It is clear that the president was emboldened to take this decision in part because those who will become its casualties are poor people of color in Africa and Asia. This was a small price to pay for rewarding a favored band of fundamentalists for their loyalty and silence during the campaign.

At the Epicenter of the Global AIDS Pandemic

The gag rule suggests even deadlier future policies against what may become the defining human struggle of the new century, the fight for Africans' right to health, indeed, to life. While many global issues are important in United States relations with Africa, no issue is of greater immediate importance than HIV/AIDS. Addressing the AIDS pandemic is not just a question of what to do, but of whether members of the international community—especially the United States—are committed to do all that is necessary to defeat the spread of AIDS in Africa.

During the past two decades, 17 million people have died in Africa due to AIDS-related illnesses. Africans infected with HIV had been deemed "untreatable" because of the artificially high prices of the anti-AIDS medications that became available five years ago. Now, responding to sharply falling AIDS drug prices brought on by competition from developing-country producers of generic versions, by African government moves to ignore patent rights to save lives, and by militant activism in the West—home to the world's largest and richest drug companies—public policymakers the world over are under pressure to produce a plan to stop the AIDS pandemic.

The World AIDS Conference in Durban, South Africa in July 2000 and the African Development Forum in Addis Ababa, Ethiopia in December has increased public attention about the pandemic, both globally and within Africa. News reports stressed not only the overwhelmingly disproportionate effect of AIDS on Africa, but also the failure of the international community to respond with more than token action. Drug companies were targeted by activists and exposed by the media for blocking efforts to provide affordable treatment drugs to combat the effects of AIDS. The "Statement of Concern on Women and HIV/AIDS" issued at the conference drew particular attention to the significance of gender inequalities in the spread of the disease, and to the fact that women and girls are placed at greatest risk of contracting it because of these disparities. But whether there is real progress during the year will depend on:

• the extent to which other African countries emulate Senegal and Uganda in putting into effect comprehensive AIDS prevention programs that combine access to condoms, sex education, treatment of opportunistic infections, safe injections, counseling, testing, and efforts to prevent mother-to-child transmission of HIV with highly visible political leadership and partnerships with civil society;

• if wealthy countries and multilateral agencies even approach the $3 billion a year estimated to be needed for HIV prevention, and the $4.5 billion a year for treatment (current funding levels are probably less than 10 percent of this for prevention, and almost none for treatment);

• if drug companies and the international community can be pressured to respond to the demand to reduce the prices of AIDS medicines to a level commensurate with their production costs.

The epicenter of the AIDS pandemic is Africa; the region with the next-highest infection rate is the Caribbean. In the United States, HIV/AIDS infection rates are increasing mainly among young men and women of color. Although AIDS is a global threat that knows no borders and does not discriminate by race, at present it is mainly killing Black people. And that is the cruel truth about why the world has failed to respond with dispatch.

This global crisis poses the question of how much inequality the United States is prepared to accept in the world and the obvious corollary: Do Americans believe that Africa is part of their common humanity? But to see how much inequality the United States government is prepared to accept globally, one only has to look at how much inequality it accepts at home.

The glacial pace of the international response to AIDS has exposed an entrenched racial double standard. As Dr. Peter Piot of the UN AIDS program remarked just before the Durban World AIDS Conference, "If this would have happened . . . with white people, the reaction would have been different."

The AIDS crisis in Africa is a stark reminder of the racial double standard that has marginalized African lives for the past 500 years. This double standard divides the world between rich and poor, white and Black. The past five centuries have brought not only progress, but also considerable suffering—and Africa has suffered disproportionately, and still does. The consequences of slavery, colonialism, and imperialism have kept Africa underdeveloped and poor, although African leaders are certainly not blameless. Now AIDS threatens Africa's very survival.

Facing the Crisis

The Bush administration has entered office at a moment of truth in the global struggle against HIV/AIDS. For Africa, the question of how the poor can get cheaper, safer, and more effective medicines is vital. What steps can the United States take?

The Clinton administration's proposal in August 2000 to lend Africa $1 billion annually at commercial rates for the purchase of antiretroviral drugs was a cruel hoax and a vivid example of government subsidized corporate greed. The plan sought to protect American pharmaceutical companies that were threatened by African rights under the World Trade Organization's (WTO) rules to pursue parallel imports and compulsory licensing of anti-AIDS drugs. But the plan showed that the United States government was prepared to push Africa further into debt to prevent Africans from purchasing cheaper drugs from Brazil or India or from licensing local firms to produce generic versions at home. Some of the World

Bank's anti-AIDS programs are largely financed along similar lines, causing some countries, such as Malawi, to reject them as worse than unsustainable. As Peter Walshe of the University of Notre Dame wrote in the February 2001 issue of *Common Sense,* "One is hard pressed to imagine a more cynical example of usury—the sin of lending surplus funds to take advantage of another's disadvantage."

The initial steps of the Bush White House have been no better. Within days of issuing the gag rule, the president expanded his assault on global public health by initiating a review of a May 2000 Clinton executive order mandating that the United States not challenge African countries seeking to exercise their rights to obtain cheaper versions of essential medications still under United States patent. (Clinton issued the order to support Al Gore's presidential bid after anti-AIDS activists targeted Gore's early campaign rallies.) Following a storm of protest, the White House announced that it would not reverse the executive order at this time.

One way in which elected officials can begin to address the pandemic is to dedicate a modest 5 percent of the budget surplus—approximately $9.5 billion in 2001—to a global health emergency fund. This would still fall short of what is needed, but it would be a leap above the paltry $325 million the United States is providing for AIDS efforts worldwide. Such funding will be necessary to help finance the acquisition of AIDS medications, either through bulk-purchasing mechanisms used for international vaccine programs, or through regional and national mechanisms. In any case, purchases should be from the safest and cheapest source available, regardless of patents (which would require a major policy shift by Washington). Such a policy will ensure that prices continue to fall to levels realistically accessible to African countries.

Life After Debt

The other key elements of an appropriate United States policy response to Africa would include the cancellation of African countries' bilateral debts to the United States and a leadership role in pressing for the outright cancellation of Africa's debts to other creditors, especially international financial institutions and European governments. The average African government spends more annually to finance its foreign debts than on national health care, and many spend more on debt servicing than on health and education combined. Zambia spends 40 percent of its total revenue on debt payments, while Cameroon, Guinea, Senegal, and Malawi all spend between 25 and 35 percent of theirs in the same manner.

These are mostly illegitimate foreign debts, contracted during the Cold War by unrepresentative governments from Western creditors that sought to buy geopolitical loyalties, not to finance development in countries previously set back by Western colonialism. They beg the question: Who owes whom?

Early gains in health care in the 1960s have been all but negated by the free-market reforms imposed by international creditors beginning in the 1980s.

The "one-size-fits-all" structural adjustment policies that African countries were forced to implement generally included currency devaluations, reductions in government spending (slashing public investments in health and education), privatization of many government services, and a focus on export-oriented agricultural development undermining food self-sufficiency. The AIDS pandemic now finds African states unable to cope.

At the end of 2000, the debt burden remained a pervasive obstacle to Africa's capacity to deal with other issues, despite additional relief won from creditors. The $34 billion package announced under the Heavily Indebted Poor Countries (HIPC) initiative included $25 billion for 18 African countries, almost half the outstanding debt owed by those countries. HIPC is the predominant international approach to debt relief and poses as a scheme to reduce the debt of world's most impoverished countries to "sustainable" levels by offering deep cuts in their total debt stock (including that held by the international financial institutions, governments, and private creditors) and pegging future payments to projected export earnings. The program is conditioned, however, on the lengthy implementation of economic austerity measures. In reality, HIPC seeks to protect creditors by using formulas designed to extract the maximum possible in debt payments from the world's poorest economies, and by continuing to use debt as leverage to prescribe economic policies for African countries.

Overall, the creditors' announcements of progress have satisfied neither debtor countries nor activists engaged on the issue, because their programs do not provide sustainable solutions. In fact, HIPC should be pronounced dead.

A continent–wide meeting of debt-cancellation activists in Dakar, Senegal in December 2000 called not only for cancellation of illegitimate debts but also for reparations from rich countries for damage to Africa. Worldwide, the demand is rising for a new mechanism to deal with the debt. In September, 2000 UN Secretary General Kofi Annan called for the immediate suspension of all debt payments by HIPC countries and others that should be added to the list, and for an independent body—not controlled by creditor countries—to consider new ways to address the debt. Substantial debt cancellation would not only free up resources for public investments in health infrastructure and education, but would liberate African countries from the imperial economic dictates of the international financial institutions, which currently undermine democratic development. It would also restore commercial creditworthiness to countries still requiring a mix of grant and loan financing for long-term development efforts. The cancellation of German debts after World War II, or those of Poland toward the end of the Cold War, are examples of previous Western willingness to provide a new lease on economic life to select deeply indebted states.

Dangerous Liaisons

While most African countries are not at war, the trauma of those that are embroiled in conflict touches the entire continent. Fragile cease-fires punctuated by episodes of violence, rather than open war, prevail in earlier conflict zones in West Africa (for example, Sierra Leone and the Casamance region of Senegal). A peace treaty between Ethiopia and Eritrea, to end the 1998 border dispute that had escalated into a massive war claiming tens of thousands of lives, was finally signed at the end of 2000, and deployment of UN observers began. The largest interlinked set of unresolved conflicts in Africa today includes Angola in west central Africa; the Democratic Republic of Congo in the heart of the continent; Burundi and Rwanda in the Great Lakes region (tying in not only to eastern Congo but also to Uganda and to Sudan); and the perennial war in Sudan itself.

If Secretary of State Powell is serious about contributing to peace in Africa, the administration needs to give new and substantial financial, diplomatic, and security support to African and UN peacemaking efforts endorsed by the Organization of African Unity (OAU) and legitimate subregional organizations. There should also be immediate restrictions on arms transfers to African countries, and greater public scrutiny of all American military training and education activities in Africa and for Africans in the United States. The Bush administration's intention to continue the Clinton policy of training and equipping select African forces as a way to avoid sharing greater responsibility for international peace efforts in Africa risks turning an unaccountable and unreformed Nigerian military into Africa's Gurkhas. And the administration's evident interest in Sudan could actually jeopardize a democratic solution to the conflict, if military measures are mistakenly given more weight than diplomacy and economic pressures, especially against foreign oil companies now financing Khartoum's war.

The African Century

Despite the severe challenges Africa faces—or perhaps because of them and their centrality to global progress—there is no reason to despair of the continent's prospects for transformation in the twenty first century. For American and international engagement with Africa to have the most positive impact, however, much greater leadership is required from African countries themselves. A number of developments suggest such leadership is forthcoming. The heads of state of three of Africa's regional powers—Nigeria, South Africa, and Algeria—have been drafting what they call Africa's Millennium Plan, an effort to promote a continent-wide consensus on development and security priorities and on mechanisms for financing Africa's economic growth while solving its debt crisis. The plan is likely to emphasize strengthening regional institutions (in which they constitute dominant powers). Another initiative, sponsored by Libya's Muammar Qaddafi, proposes the establishment of a continental United States of Africa with mechanisms for cooperation similar to institutions of the European Union.

These and other efforts reveal just how acutely aware African leaders are of the weak positions they will continue to occupy on the global stage absent a greater collective voice. In addition, African civil society actors—from human rights organizations to African entrepreneurs—are tackling immediate problems such as AIDS education, constitutional reform, poverty eradication, and conflict resolution. Nearly every African conflict has a peace plan and process crafted by Africans themselves, but which lack adequate international support.

The promotion of peace, democracy, and development in Africa is necessary and vital to combat the global threats that will challenge the United States in the century ahead. The attainment of these goals is desirable on their own merits, because of the economic and social benefits the United States will realize. These will include savings from reduced expenditures on emergency relief activities, the development of regional institutions able to cooperate more productively with the United States on various international issues, and expanding markets and investment opportunities that will help the United States sustain its economy while supporting African economic growth. Withdrawal, or neglect, would aid the establishment of a global apartheid that creates economic, social, and security disparities throughout the world and within countries along the color line—and that would put American democracy itself at risk.

The Implications of the (Second) Bush Presidency

Looking at the lineup of policymakers responsible for global affairs and Africa policies, it would be unrealistic to expect much progress in United States policy toward Africa were it not for the rise in public activism on African and Africa-related issues such as AIDS and foreign debt.

President George W. Bush has little foreign policy experience and, as with domestic policy, is likely to follow the lead of his vice president. Vice President Dick Cheney's perspective on Africa is illustrated by his support for keeping Nelson Mandela in prison and his opposition to sanctions against apartheid South Africa while he was a member of Congress. More recently, as CEO of Halliburton, the world's largest oil services company, he was complicit in lining the pockets of the dictatorship of the late General Sani Abacha in Nigeria. National Security Adviser Condoleezza Rice was, until this year, a director of Chevron, another oil company that buttressed military rule in Nigeria and even hired the regime's soldiers for crowd-control work—work that including firing on unarmed protesters at the sites of its operations in Nigeria. (A Chevron oil tanker even bears her name.) With Bush himself coming from the oil industry, oil is likely to top the list of United States interests in Africa as defined by the Bush "oiligarchy."

Neither Rice nor Secretary of State Colin Powell, both African Americans, demonstrated a particular interest in or special knowledge of Africa. Moreover, both Powell and Rice are loyal Republicans with a shared orientation toward international affairs that derives from a narrow, militaristic understanding of security. They are also unilateralists at a time when the need in Africa is for multilateral support for peace and security.

The person chosen to become the top Africa policymaker at the State Department, Walter Kansteiner III, comes out of the right-wing Institute on Religion and Democracy in Washington, where he criticized mainline Christian denominations for supporting democratic change in apartheid South Africa. A commodity trader and adviser on privatization in Africa, Kansteiner also served in the White House under Bush's father. Like Cheney, he opposed sanctions against apartheid South Africa years after they were in place, and as late as 1990 considered the prodemocracy movement in South Africa, led by Nelson Mandela's African National Congress (ANC), to be unrepresentative of most South Africans. With analytical skills like those, he appears singularly unqualified for the job except that he fits the profile of many new Bush staff: conservative ideologues who served Bush's father.

Development Deficit

In December 2001, the World Health Organization (WHO) Commission on Macroeconomics and Health released the results of its two-year study showing that scaling up global investment in health would produce enormous economic gains. The report provides a wealth of supporting arguments in favor of investment in public goods such as health, education, and other infrastructure as essential prerequisites for development on all fronts. At the beginning of 2002, however, there were few signs that there would be breakthroughs in the continuing debates on trade, aid, and debt.

Meanwhile, the International Monetary Fund announced that estimates of the economic growth rate for the African continent in 2001, with the added impact of September 11 and the global recession, fell to 3.5 percent (3.1 percent in sub-Saharan Africa). Prospects for recovery in 2002 were not strong.

A multiyear UN effort to promote new thinking about global financing for development culminated in March 2002 in Monterrey, Mexico. The framework for the conference contained many common elements with the New Economic Partnership for Africa's Development (NEPAD) framework adopted by African leaders in 2001: new "ownership" of economic development plans by developing countries, mobilizing domestic resources, "untying" of aid in favor of support for agreed-upon plans, regional cooperation, greater access to markets in developed countries, increases in both donor support and private capital flows, and debt reduction.

Behind the bland language of these compromise documents lie substantial disagreements on particular issues. For example, Washington and the international financial institutions continue to stress trade liberalization, along with other measures to attract foreign investment, as the high road to development. Yet while the pressure on developing countries for more liberalization continues unabated, opening rich country markets remains a pious wish. As IMF director Horst Koehler stressed in January 2002, rich countries still spend hundreds of billions of dollars on subsidies "in areas where developing countries have a comparative advantage—as in agriculture, processed foods, textiles and clothing, and light manufactures."

Meanwhile, African exports continue to be concentrated on vulnerable primary commodities. High-profile initiatives such as the US Africa Growth and Opportunity Act have had little impact on this pattern. The second report on the act released in January, 2002 by the US International Trade Commission, for example, shows significant increases in US imports from Africa, but these were overwhelmingly dominated by oil and other energy-related products.

Disagreements also exist around the question of how much aid is dispersed, and who makes such decisions. European countries and the World Bank have joined UN agencies and African countries in calling for significant increases in official development assistance, arguing that such investments in health, education, and other sectors are indispensable requirements for economic advance and poverty alleviation.

UN Secretary General Kofi Annan has won significant support from other "donors" for the goal of doubling official development assistance. US Treasury Secretary Paul O'Neill has joined critics of the conventional development model in calling for a shift from loans to grants to finance development in the poorest countries. At the same time, however, O'Neill has seized every opportunity, including the World Economic Forum in New York, to reiterate Washington's hard-line refusal to accept even a rhetorical commitment to providing increased funds.

Despite the Monterrey Consensus "noting with concern current estimates of dramatic shortfalls in resources required to achieve the internationally agreed development goals," debate in Washington remains mired in the stereotype of aid as optional and wasteful charity. Without a shift in paradigm (partially visible in the debate over the global health fund), public investment for global and African development is likely to face further setbacks rather than gains in Washington.

The question of debt reduction is also a source of considerable controversy—despite claims of success by creditors for their Heavily Indebted Poor Countries (HIPC) initiative for debt reduction, the IMF estimated that Africa's debt service payments would only go as low as 17.1 percent of export earnings in 2001 (down from 20.3 percent in 1999, before rising again to 18.4 percent in 2002.) This is still a crippling economic burden, as African leaders as well as debt cancellation campaigners continue to stress. The overwhelming majority of the debt is owed to the World Bank and the IMF. But neither the international financial institutions nor the rich creditor countries gave any indication they were willing to consider more than marginal adjustments in the HIPC program.

Conflict Resolution and Democracy

In most African countries the structural violence of disease and economic injustice posed much larger threats to human security than the reality or risk of open conflict. One principal zone of instability and humanitarian need on the continent continues to be the region from Angola in west central Africa through the Democratic Republic of the Congo, Burundi, Rwanda, and portions of Uganda to Sudan in the northeast.

Peace processes with very uncertain outcomes are underway with limited international support in the Democratic Republic of the Congo and Burundi. But both countries remained among the most serious humanitarian emergencies in the world, together with Sudan and Angola.

Despite a limited cease-fire in the Nuba Mountains region in Sudan at the beginning of the year, and increased civil society pressure for peace in Angola, the prospects for a breakthrough to a genuine peace process in 2002 were not high in either country. Major outside powers seemed more likely to show interest in expanded oil production in both countries than in the search for peace. Implementation of sanctions against "conflict diamonds" remained inconsistent. Trade in diamonds, timber, and valuable minerals such as coltan continued to provide resources for conflict in Angola, central Africa, and the Mano River area in West Africa.

Elections in a number of African countries during 2001, including Benin, Chad, Gambia, Madagascar, Uganda, and Zambia, added to skepticism about manipulation of the process by incumbents, violence, and other barriers to democratic participation. In each case internal and external criticism was vocal, but the threat of open internal conflict was avoided.

With Kenya due to hold elections before the end of 2002, and Nigeria early in 2003, the danger is great that repression, manipulation, and other tensions leading up to elections could provoke escalated conflict. This would have enormous consequences not only for the countries themselves but also for their regions within the continent, and for Africa's efforts to address continent-wide problems.

In Nigeria, internal violence due to multiple causes is rising in this pre-election year. Instead of promoting security, the Nigerian military has contributed its own share of violence against civilians. Many question the capacity of President Olusegun Obasanjo's government to maintain stability and deliver on the promises of democracy. Kenyans meanwhile fear a repetition of the last elections in 1997, when government-instigated violence and opposition disunity helped return incumbent President Daniel Arap Moi to power.

Prodemocracy activists in these three countries and around the continent are profoundly skeptical of political elites who offer nationalist rhetoric, managed elections, and violence against opponents as a substitute for democracy. But they are also critical of outside powers for being inconsistent in support for conflict resolution and democracy. To cite only a few examples, Western critiques have been nearly inaudible with respect to the lack of democracy in Egypt (Washington's favored aid partner), Sudan (being wooed as an oil-producer and security ally), and Zambia (with an election widely regarded as fraudulent).

Yet with the US and other outside powers preoccupied with the threat from global terrorism following September 11, focus on resolving Africa's internal conflicts may well rank even lower on the agenda of the "international community." Even if overt US intervention does not occur, the tendency to reinforce selected partners and ignore human rights abuses under the guise of fighting terrorism is certain to be powerful.

Chapter 16

Praying for a Revolution

Reverend Paul Scott

If you go to any Black church on any given Sunday, you can bet your last money that the topic of the sermon will not deviate much from the familiar script that you have heard a hundred times (otherwise known as "the same ol', same ol' ").

The pastor will get a chorus of "uh huh's" as he chastises the congregation for being "back biters" and "sneakin' around." (Well!) The mothers of the church will give a loud "Amen!" as he tells the teenagers to "cut off that rap music and pull their pants up." (Go 'head and tell it!) Tears will start rollin' as he tells the congregation that although they are used and abused and 'buked and scorned that there is a "bright side over Jord'n." (Y'all don't hear me!) The reason that these subjects are preached so frequently is because they do not offend white folks and do not challenge the white power structure.

But what about those of us who want freedom instead of fighting with our brothers and sisters over foolishness? What about those of us who are more concerned about pursuing liberation than pursuing someone else's spouse? Is there a word from heaven for us?

I never understood how people can praise the Lord on the inside of a church while drug dealers and prostitutes are on the steps on the outside. Don't they need a word from God, too? Historically, at its best, the Black church has been a source of strength for our people, but at its worst it has been used as an agency of social control by the white power structure. If a white man wanted to influence the actions of the Black community, instead of dealing with the masses, he would merely gain the confidence of the preacher and the congregation would follow "as sheep led to a slaughter."

What if the pastor would stand up every Sunday morning and preach against the white supremacist system with the same energy (and volume) that he preaches about what Black folks are doing wrong? What if he challenged the congregation to go out and fight for freedom after each service? How long would it be before changes happened in that neighborhood—or that city?

Now it is not unusual for the church to get a little "Blacker" during white-sanctioned events like Black history month. One Sunday out of the year, Deacon Frye may wear a kufi and Rev. Jones may wear his kente cloth robe and talk about how we need the "ole time religion that freed us from slav'ry and 'pression." But why can't we have that every Sunday in a Black church full of Black people? The Black church must teach our history in and out of season, and not just our post-1865 history, but the true history of the African people depicted in the scriptures.

What effect would it have on the Junior Usher board as they matured into Black men and women if they were constantly told that the people in the Bible were African people, their ancestors? I doubt if they would join the ranks of the brothers and sisters who started off singing in the youth choir, but took a wrong turn and found themselves in jail.

Some preachers have attempted to reach out to the hip hop generation by imitating the fashions and slang of hip hop artists, but if they still have pictures of a white "Jesus" in their churches it is symbol without substance. They should return their FUBU jackets and put their black pinstriped double-breasted suits back on. There are gospel artists who have done a good job mixing hip hop and gospel. But if your subject matter is still based on Eurocentric slave theology, it doesn't matter how funky your beat is—you are just singing loud, and saying nothing. The young people today have been exposed to so many concepts via the media and the Internet that you cannot tell them anything that sounds good and expect them to buy it. Can you tell the young brothers selling drugs on the corner that they are going to hell for killing our people, while at the

same time saying that the white men who murdered our ancestors
are up in heaven?

The Black church is in need of a Revolution. To be a follower
of Yeshua (Jesus), the Black, revolutionary Messiah, one must be in
a constant struggle against the forces of oppression. If you are not
involved in the struggle for liberation, as the scriptures teach, you
are like the "salt that has lost its savor." We cannot mute our voices
because we're afraid that someone might accuse us of preaching
hate.

What the Black Church Must Do

The condition of the Black church in the twenty-first century can
be best summed up in the words of a friend of mine who recently
left the church. "Brother, it isn't the religion that turns people off,
it's the representatives." Or to borrow from the hip hoppers, "Y'all
ain't representin'; y'all ain't keepin' it real."

The Black church is at a crucial point in its history, whether it
will be that "pillar of strength" which it was at its apex or if it will
remain the Sunday morning social club that many have become
since the civil rights era. There are several things that the church
must do this year in order to "seek that which was lost" and not
lose even more in the process.

First, the church must become more "user friendly." Too
many times, instead of spreading the Gospel, we are more interested in promoting the idea that the spirit of God only dwells in
"my church." So we limit our whole religious experience to a two
hour period in a building on Sunday morning instead of manifest-
ing it in our ways and actions. Our spirituality becomes a ritual instead of a way of life, which is totally against the teachings of
Yeshua (misnamed Jesus). The Messiah was a liberator and a revolutionary, and those who follow him must be involved in the uplift-
ing of the African American community. I never understood how
people could be "testifying" inside the church while "lost" brothers and sisters sit on the front steps. The Word must be brought to
them, as well. No one has the right to copyright a religion; it must
be open to all who seek truth.

And while many have rightly seen the mission of the church in the twenty-first century to reach the young hip hop generation, that doesn't mean that every Sunday morning service should become "Hip Hop Central." I always tell folks if I want to hear DMX, I'll go and buy a DMX CD. Many people who are "saved" and feel that they are above secular music, compensate their urge to "still get down" by playing "gospel rap." However, just because someone gives a "shout out to Jesus" does not make the song spiritually edifying. A spiritual song should inspire listeners to, borrowing from the old Goodie Mob lyrics, "Get up, get out, and do somethin'."

Also, when some get too "holy" to watch sitcoms, they trade them in for so-called gospel plays like, "Mama, When Will I Find Somebody to Treat Me Right?" As the scriptures teach, we are too quick to go after "things that do not profit," or raise our level of consciousness in the name of religion.

Next, the pastors must "feed the sheep" with knowledge instead of playing the classic "I know something you don't know" game. Despite all the Biblical knowledge some pastors possess, their messages to the people rarely surpass "Jesus loves me, this I know, for the Bible tells me so" or stories from the big, blue, children's Bible storybook with all those pictures of white folks in it that many of us read in Sunday school. The subject matter must change. What effect would it have on the young folks in the congregation if Pastor Jones told them that the Messiah was a Black man and his message of liberation is relevant for the struggle of the dispossessed? How many more sermons must we sit through with a pastor telling poor people in the back they should suffer on earth (not for speaking truth to power as Yeshua did, but just for the sake of sufferin') while the big money folks who sit up front drive to church in Cadillacs, every Sunday.

Most importantly, what is needed in the church is what I call an "African Reformation Movement." There have been reformation movements initiated by Europeans, but since we've been taught that Christianity is a gift from the white man, some of us have not felt that we have the spiritual authority to change a thing. We have accepted the religion as is.

Yet, what is referred to as "Christianity" in its essence has just as much connection to Africa as any other religion practiced by Black folks. Leaders in the African Reformation Movement will boldly state that most of the people in the Bible were Black people, and Black churches would be urged to remove the blue-eyed, blond-haired pictures of the white man posing as "Jesus" and replace them with pictures of Yeshua, the Black revolutionary Messiah.

We as a people have been too quick to give away everything that the European claims is theirs: religion, land, culture. This is especially exemplified in popular music such as rock and roll, jazz, and hip hop. A hundred years from now, I wouldn't be surprised if the history books record that Vanilla Ice discovered hip hop, Kenny G discovered jazz, and Michael Jackson was a white man who revolutionized music videos. We must keep what is ours very close to our hearts and put it in the memory of our children.

The call for an African Reformation Movement in the Black church must come from those inside of the church, and not from those on the outside looking in. Unfortunately, most of the criticism of the Church (constructive and otherwise) comes from folks who wouldn't set foot in a church even if Marcus Garvey was preachin' and the Black Panther Party served as ushers.

Yet, church folks must take the chip off their shoulders when someone asks honest questions regarding "Christianity." Every question is not a "diss" and should require a deeper response then "there y'all go again, messin' with my Jesus."

If church folks want to stop being referred to as those who follow "white man's religion," they must stop following the white man's religion—the Eurocentric version of Christianity. The stereotype in some Afrocentric circles that those Black folks that go to church do so "cause they just don't know any better" must be broken. This will happen when the church begins to see the Messiah as more than a picture on a wall, and embraces the message of liberation found in the scriptures.

Even though the Black church has been historically resistant to change—look how long it took choirs to even occasionally decorate their robes with kente cloth—I believe that if enough church folks want change, change will happen. As Sam Cooke beautifully sang years ago, "it's been a long time comin' but I know change gonna come."

Index

About the Contributors

Amiri Baraka (LeRoi Jones) was born in Newark, New Jersey in 1934. After attending Howard University in Washington, DC, he served in the United States Air Force. In the late fifties, he settled in New York's Greenwich Village. He became nationally prominent in 1964, with the New York production of his Obie Award winning play, *Dutchman*. After the death of Malcolm X he became a Black Nationalist, moving first to Harlem and then back home to Newark. In the mid-1970s, abandoning Cultural Nationalism, he became a Third World Marxist-Leninist. After teaching for twenty years in the Department of Africana Studies at the State University of New York (SUNY)-Stony Brook, he retired in 1999. He lives with his wife, the poet Amina Baraka, in Newark.

Salih Booker is executive director of Africa Action, which was recently created by the merger of three related nonprofit organizations: the Africa Fund, the American Committee on Africa, and the Africa Policy Information Center. Over the last fifteen years he has worked for the Council on Foreign Relations Africa Studies Program, the Ford Foundation, and for the United Nations. He has published articles and opinion pieces for the *Washington Post, Los Angeles Times, Boston Globe, The Nation, Current History, Africa News Service, Africa Report, TransAfrica Forum Journal,* and various other US and international publications.

Todd Steven Burroughs is a freelance journalist/researcher/consultant based in the Washington, DC metropolitan area. He is completing the research stages of a biography on death row journalist Mumia Abu-Jamal.

Yvonne Bynoe is president and co-founder of Urban Think Tank, Inc., an organization that critically analyzes the political, economic, and cultural issues that affect rap music, hip hop culture, and its fans. Ms. Bynoe is a graduate of Howard University, and earned a law degree from Fordham University.

Ron Daniels was an independent candidate for President of the United States in 1992. He served as executive director of the National Rainbow Coalition in 1987, and deputy campaign manager for Jesse Jackson's 1988 presidential campaign. He is a scholar-activist who has taught history, political science, and black studies at several colleges, including Cornell University and The College of Wooster. He is the convenor of the State of the Black World conference, and executive director of the Center for Constitutional Rights.

Angela Y. Davis is known internationally for her ongoing work to combat all forms of oppression in the US and abroad. Over the years, she has been active as a student, teacher, writer, scholar, and activist/organizer. She is currently a tenured professor in the History of Consciousness Department at the University of California, Santa Cruz. A member of the advisory board of the Prison Activist Resource Center, Davis is working on a comparative study of women's imprisonment in the US, the Netherlands, and Cuba. In 1997, Davis helped found Critical Resistance, a national organization dedicated to dismantling the Prison Industrial Complex (PIC), a concept she developed.

Bill Fletcher, Jr. is President of TransAfrica Forum, the nation's leading lobby on issues relating to Africa and the Caribbean.

Jennifer Hamer is a former National Co-Chair of the Black Radical Congress, and former editor of *BRC Today: National Newsletter of the Black Radical Congress*. She is an associate professor of Sociology at Wayne State University. She has authored several publications on the experiences of African American families, including *What it Means to be Daddy: Black Fathers Who Live Away from Their Children* (Columbia University Press, 2001).

bell hooks is the author of numerous critically acclaimed books on the politics of race, gender, class, and culture. She lectures frequently in the United States and abroad.

Joy James is professor of Africana Studies at Brown University. She is the author of *Shadowboxing, Resisting State Violence,* and *Transcending the Talented Tenth*. Her recent editorial work includes: *States of Confinement, The Black Feminist Reader* (co-edited with T. Denean Sharpley-Whiting), and the forthcoming anthology by political prisoners, *American Prison Notebooks.*

Clarence Lang was a member of the Black Radical Congress National Council, and a participant in the BRC Youth Caucus (1998-2001). He is a Ph.D. candidate in history at the University of Illinois at Urbana-Champaign. He has written and co-authored several articles on contemporary Black social movements and political culture.

Julianne Malveaux, an MIT-trained economist, is a writer and syndicated columnist whose thoughts on national affairs, the American workplace, and the economy appear each week in more than twenty newspapers nationally, including the *Los Angeles Times, San Francisco Examiner, San Francisco Sun Reporter, Oregonian,* and the *Detroit News.* Dr. Malveaux writes a monthly column for *USA Today* and *Black Issues in Higher Education.* She is also a frequent contributor to national magazines such as *Essence, Ms., The Crisis, Black Enterprise,* and *Progressive..*

Manning Marable is Professor of History and Political Science and the Director of the Institute for Research in African-American Studies at Columbia University. He is co-founder of the Black Radical Congress, a national network of African American activists. He is the author of 13 books, including *Black Leadership* (Columbia University Press, 1998). Among his current projects is the Malcolm X Project, where he is writing a biography of the famed leader's life.

Sonia Sanchez's poems depict the struggles between Black people and white people, between men and women, and between cultures. She is innovative in her use of language and structure, sometimes using Black speech in her poetry. Sanchez is a recipient of the Robert Frost Medal in Poetry (2000), one of the highest honors awarded to a nationally recognized poet. Among her books are *Under a Soprano Sky, Does Your House Have Lions?, Shake Loose My Skin: New and Selected Poems,* and *Homegirls & Handgrenades* (1984), which won an American Book Award from the Before Columbus Foundation.

Paul Scott, 35, is an ordained Baptist minister and founder of the Durham NC-based New Righteous Movement. Scott is also a community activist, writer, and lecturer. He has written articles for many Black newspapers and websites, and is a frequent guest on radio talk shows.

Johnita Scott-Obadele has served as Director of the Institute for Social and Educational Development, Inc. (ISED) in Baton Rouge, Louisiana since 1975. Scott-Obadele was the National Co-chair Coordinator of N'COBRA (1993-98), and Managing Editor of ENCOBRA Magazine. She earned her Master's Degree in Education at Indiana University, Bloomington.

Charles Simmons is currently a member of the advisory editorial board of the *Michigan Citizen Newspaper* and the board of directors of the Detroiters Working for Environmental Justice. He is a professor of English Language and Literature at Eastern Michigan University.

Alice A. Tait is a professor at Central Michigan University. She earned her PhD in mass communications research and theory from Bowling Green University. Tait, with J.A. Barber, is co-editor of *African Americans and New Communications Technology* (Greenwood Publishing Group, Inc.). Her articles have appeared in a number of publications, including *The Negro Educational Review, Michigan Academician, Handbook on Mass Media in the United States,* and *Western Journal of Black Studies.*

Phill Wilson is founder and executive director of the African American AIDS Policy and Training Institute and the National Black Lesbian & Gay Leadership Forum. Currently a columnist for *POZ* and *Arise* magazines, Wilson's articles have appeared in popular publications such as the *Los Angeles Times,* the *Los Angeles Weekly, Essence, New York Times, Newsweek,* and *Ebony.* He lives in Los Angeles with his two teenage nephews.

About South End Press

South End Press is a nonprofit, collectively run book publisher with more than 200 titles in print. Since our founding in 1977, we have tried to meet the needs of readers who are exploring, or are already committed to, the politics of radical social change. Our goal is to publish books that encourage critical thinking and constructive action on the key political, cultural, social, economic, and ecological issues shaping life in the United States and in the world. In this way, we hope to give expression to a wide diversity of democratic social movements and to provide an alternative to the products of corporate publishing.

Through the Institute for Social and Cultural Change, South End Press works with other political media projects—Alternative Radio; Speakout, a speakers' bureau; and *Z Magazine*—to expand access to information and critical analysis.

To order books, please send a check or money order to: South End Press, 7 Brookline Street, #1, Cambridge, MA 02139-4146. To order by credit card, call 1-800-533-8478. Please include $3.50 for postage and handling for the first book and 50 cents for each additional book.

Write or email southend@southendpress.org for a free catalog, or visit our website at www.southendpress.org.

Related Titles from South End Press

Ain't I A Woman
bell hooks

Black Looks: Race and Representation
bell hooks

Breaking Bread: Insurgent Black Intellectual Life
bell hooks and Cornel West

Sisters of the Yam: Black Women and Self-Recovery
bell hooks

Yearning: Race, Gender, and Cultural Politics
bell hooks

Race in the Global Era: African Americans at the Millennium
Clarence Lusane

How Capitalism Underdeveloped Black America (updated edtion)
Manning Marable

Black Liberation in Conservative America
Manning Marable

From Civil Rights to Black Liberation
William W. Sales, Jr.